Michael Spira was born in 1944, educated at Stowe School, and qualified at St Bartholomew's Hospital, London. He has written several books and many articles on health and medical topics. He broadcasts regularly as a radio doctor and makes occasional television appearances. He has lectured widely on the subject of obesity and slimming.

He is married and has two children.

THE
3D
SLIMMING
DIET

Michael Spira

CORGI BOOKS

THE 3D SLIMMING DIET

A CORGI BOOK 0 552 12366 8

First publication in Great Britain

PRINTING HISTORY

Corgi edition published 1984

This book is set in 10/11 Baskerville

Corgi Books are published by Transword Publishers Ltd.,
Century House, 61-63 Uxbridge Road, Ealing, London W5 5SA

Made and printed in Great Britain by
Hunt Barnard Printing Ltd., Aylesbury, Bucks.

Contents

Preface

This book is intended for two groups of people.

The first is those who seek an effective and *medically approved* diet which will help them to slim *healthily*.

The second is those who are not necessarily overweight but who seek a healthy and well-balanced everyday diet which will help to reduce the risk of acquiring coronary heart disease, the chief killer disease today. An added benefit is a probable reduction in the risk of cancer, especially of the bowel and the breast.

Acknowledgements

The list of calorie and cholesterol values of foods in this book are taken, with kind permission of the publisher, mainly from McCance and Widdowson's *The Composition of Foods* – the Medical Research Council's Special Report No 297 (the fourth and revised edition) by A. A. Paul and D. A. T. Southgate, published by HM Stationery Office. The figures for the saturated fat content of foods are calculations which I have made based on data in the same publication, and any inaccuracies are entirely my own responsibility.

The tables of maximum desirable weights for adults are adapted from the Metropolitan Life Insurance Company 1960 tables. The tables of the ranges of heights and weights for boys and girls are adapted, with kind permission of the authors and editor, from Tanner J. M., Whitehouse R. H. and Takaishi M. Standards from birth to maturity for height, weight, height velocity and weight velocity: British Children, 1965, part 2, *Arch. Dis. Childh.* (1866), vol 41, pages 613ff. (The original tables express heights and weights in centimetres and kilograms. For convenience I have added their equivalents in feet and inches and stones and pounds.)

Finally, I wish to record my immeasurable debt to my wife, Alison, both for her encouragement and for her written contributions. In particular, the recipes in this book (without which the book would have been of little value) I owe entirely to her. Incidentally this, rather than delusions of monarchal grandeur, accounts for the use of the pronoun *we* throughout the book.

The 3D Diet

The 3 DO's:

On the 3D Diet you DO

* lose weight safely and permanently
* something positive for your health, i.e. you reduce your risk of disease, especially coronary heart disease and some cancers
* eat nutritionally sound and balanced meals which are delicious and varied

The 3 DON'T's:

On the 3D Diet you DON'T

* eat too many calories
* eat too many saturated fats
* eat too much cholesterol

The 3 extra points:

The 3D Diet is

* approved by world health experts
* suitable for ALL the family
* easy to follow anywhere, not just at home

CHAPTER 1

The Success of the 3D Diet

The last few years has seen the publication and popularity of many widely different diets, none of which has proved to be the ideal solution for slimmers.

So why the 3D Diet? Quite simply, because it is a *successful* diet.

So, what is a successful diet?

A SUCCESSFUL DIET MUST BE ENJOYABLE

The 3D Diet is enjoyable because it does not make you go without all your favourite foods. Instead you will be shown two things. First, how to make quite small changes to your existing diet. And second, how to make low calorie and low saturated fat foods interesting and appealing.

A SUCCESSFUL DIET CAN BE FOLLOWED FOR EVER

Because the 3D Diet has tasty recipes and because it does not require you to go hungry, you can follow the diet for the rest of your life, if you wish. Remember that a weight problem needs a *permanent* solution. A question that you should always ask yourself before considering any new diet is:

Is this a diet I could stick to for the rest of my life?

The 3D Diet is one of the very few diets for which the answer is YES.

A SUCCESSFUL DIET MUST NOT BE ANTISOCIAL

Once you understand the principles of the 3D Diet you will be able to eat quite freely wherever you are, such as in a

11

restaurant, dining with friends, and so on. This is because the diet is based on everyday foods, and it is a diet that the whole family can follow.

A SUCCESSFUL DIET IS A HEALTHY, NON-FADDY DIET

The 3D Diet is a well-balanced diet which contains all the nutrients you need to help you lose weight *healthily*. Because it contains few of the unhealthy nutrients it goes even further. *It helps to reduce the risk of coronary heart disease and certain forms of cancer.*

A SUCCESSFUL DIET WORKS

This may seem too obvious to say, but the fact is that there are many diets which do *not* result in loss of weight. Happily, the 3D Diet works very successfully.

A CLOSER LOOK AT THE 3D DIET

In recent years, interest has been growing in the dietary risk factors associated with coronary heart disease – the single most common cause of middle age death in the Western world today. Both in the United Kingdom and the USA, expert committees have produced reports. The consensus is that there are two factors: overweight and cholesterol. In 1976 the Royal College of Physicians and the British Cardiac Society published a report *The Prevention of Coronary Heart Disease*. That report recommended that the total amount of fat, and especially of saturated fat (the fat which increases the level of cholesterol in the blood), in the diet should be reduced. In 1983 the same Royal College published its report on Obesity in which the same recommendation was made again. At the same time both reports also recommended the reduction of sugar in the diet.

The reasons for these recommendations are simple. Fats are the most calorific part of the diet: they contain nine calories a gram compared with four calories a gram of carbohydrates and proteins. Therefore reduce dietary fats and you reduce calories far more effectively, and with far less likelihood of hunger, than reducing the traditional target of many slimming diets, carbohydrates. Concentrate on reducing *saturated* fats in the diet and you reduce not only the consumption of calories but also the intake of the dietary ingredient which may fatally damage your heart. Reduce sugar intake and you further reduce calorie consumption without depriving your body of any other nutrients since sugar has no other nutrients.

As you can see the logical conclusion is that if you want to lose weight *and* do something positive with your diet to protect your heart you should follow a diet low in saturated fats, cholesterol and sugar. Hence the 3D Diet, which has a added bonus that, *unlike many traditional diets, hunger is rarely a problem.*

And then there is the added benefit that, according to recent evidence, a diet low in fats, especially saturated fats, may help to reduce the risk of cancer, particularly cancer of the bowel and cancer of the breast.

Ever since the diet was first tested in 1982 the success in terms of the amount of weight lost and long term maintenance of target weights has confirmed that this diet is the logical solution to the problem of overweight. Comparisons with other popular diets, such as high protein, low carbohydrate and high fibre, have shown that the 3D Diet is the most appealing and most rewarding.

It has also attracted many non-slimmers because of the health benefits of a low saturated fat diet.

One final point. This is *not* a cookery book. Rather it is a book of recipes which it is hoped will act as useful suggestions about preparing meals which, in addition to being 'slimming' and healthy, are both *varied* and *interesting*.

CHAPTER 2

Why Are People Overweight?

Why am I overweight? This is a question every overweight person asks. It is simply a question of balance.

A QUESTION OF BALANCE

If you eat more calories than your body burns up you put weight on. If you eat less than you burn up you lose weight. Now people who are naturally slim – you know the ones, they always pile their plates up high with potatoes and eat puddings *and* ice-cream *and* cheese – have one thing going for them that the rest of us haven't: their metabolism. Whenever they consume more calories than their bodies need their metabolism changes gear so that they burn up more calories. They convert excess food eaten into heat whereas the rest of us convert this into fat.

So, you are overweight because you are eating more calories than your inefficient metabolism can cope with.

Why do some people burn up fewer calories?
One theory centres around *brown fat*. Some years ago experiments showed that obese mice, when placed in cold conditions, became colder and colder whereas lean mice maintained their body temperature increasing their metabolic rate.

But it was not until the late 1970s that Foster and Frydman, two Canadians, solved the mystery of *how* lean mice increased their body temperature. They showed that the site of heat production was a specialized tissue, brown fat, found in various parts of the body, but most especially between the shoulder blades. In fat mice the brown fat produces less heat than in lean mice.

14

As brown fat is present in all warm-blooded animals, including man, the question was could this discovery be the basis of a 'breakthrough' in the battle against the bulge?

Sadly, although there is plenty of brown fat present in new-born babies there is no evidence *yet* that brown fat is important as a heat producer in adult human beings. If this is ever shown then the door will be opened to the development of a drug which will *safely* increase heat production in the brown fat of overweight people. But at present that moment is a very long way away.

'BONNY' BABIES

Fat babies tend to grow up into fat adults. One theory is that obesity in the first few months of life – remember the 'bonny baby' so beloved only a few years ago? – causes an increase in the number of fat cells in the body which as a poor adult he spends the rest of his or her life fighting to prevent being filled with fat.

MIDDLE-AGED SPREAD

Middle-aged spread is largely the result of the most obvious cause of reduced energy output – lack of exercise over a long period of time. The trouble is that it is all very well to slow down physically as you grow older providing you also eat a little less. Unfortunately most people don't. Just one slice of bread or one potato more than your body needs each day adds a few ounces of fat to your body each week, adding up to several pounds or even an extra stone each year or two.

EXERCISE

The amount of exercise that you have to take to make any appreciable difference to your weight is colossal. For example, if you walk one mile at a moderate pace you will burn up, in calorie terms, the equivalent of one slice of bread (without butter!), a cream cracker, or 30 grams (one ounce) of plain chocolate. But exercise is not entirely a waste of time. It boosts your metabolism which helps to burn up some of the calories that you have eaten. It also increases your general level of fitness, which often increases the motivation to eat less.

But some people do actually eat more than others. Why?
The reason is that a nerve centre in the brain, called the *appestat*, which controls appetite, may be damaged. For example, if solids are introduced into a baby's diet too early, the appestat becomes set at a higher level so that more food is needed to switch it off.

Another cause of damage to the appestat is bottle-feeding. When a baby's mother can see exactly how much milk there is for him and if he does not take it all she worries. She encourages him to take more than he really wants and eventually his natural reflex to stop feeding when he no longer feels hungry is surpressed. As he grows older the pressure on him to satisfy his mother's wants rather than his continues, and he is taught to 'wipe the plate clean'. He no longer responds to hunger as his sole cue to eat, nor does he respond to the satisfying of hunger as the cue to stop eating.

THE SWEET TOOTH

Sugar and sweet-tasting foods lead inevitably to a 'sweet tooth' which in turn results in the consumption of a lot of calories.

STRESS AND EMOTION

Adults who are depressed often turn to food for comfort. Stress makes some people eat more just as others may bite their nails. Many people eat simply because they are bored.

GIVING UP SMOKING

It has become almost a fact of life that giving up smoking inevitably results in putting on weight. In fact, the weight gain is the result of eating more rather than the lack of tobacco. The reason for overeating is that one addiction (nicotine) has been replaced with another (excessive eating).

There are many people who have managed to give up smoking *and* lose weight.

YOUR SLIMMING SUCCESS IS NOW AT HAND

As you can see there are many reasons for becoming overweight. Some are to do with not burning up sufficient calories. But most are to do with simply eating too much. In *Table Talk* John Seldon wrote, ''Tis not the eating, nor 'tis the drinking that is to be blamed, but the excess.'

And that is what this book is all about – cutting out the 'excess'.

And this is the reason that you will succeed in this diet. You will *not* have to cut down drastically on your food. You will *not* have to cut out all your favourite foods. Instead you will be shown how to be more moderate in all your eating so that you can cut down your calories AND still enjoy your food.

Remember, on the 3D Diet you WILL

* lose weight safely and permanently
* do something positive for your health
* eat nutritionally sound and balanced meals which are delicious and varied.

CHAPTER 3

Cholesterol and Saturated Fats

Cholesterol is a fatty substance which is present in everyone's blood. It comes either from foods rich in cholesterol, such as eggs, or is manufactured in the body from foods which contain a lot of saturated fats, the main sources being meat and dairy products. Plants, which include fruit and vegetables, contain no cholesterol and, with one or two minor exceptions, no saturated fats.

There are two types of fats – fats that are solid (at room temperature) and oils (which are liquid at room temperature). Solid fats come mainly from animal meat and dairy products whereas oils come from vegetable sources such as corn, olive, soya bean, sunflower and safflower. Both fats and oils are chemicals formed from carbon, hydrogen and oxygen. If the chemical bonds between the carbon atoms are *saturated* (that is, all the bonds are occupied by hydrogen atoms) the fats are solid; if the bonds are *unsaturated* (that is, not all the potential bonds are occupied) then the fats are liquid – in other words, they are oils. The difference between saturated and unsaturated fats is important mainly in connection with coronary heart disease and we shall look at this in more detail in the next chapter.

Fats and oils are important to us. They provide us with a source of future energy. Fats are the principal sources of some vitamins, especially vitamins A and D. Fat lines the skin which insulates the body from cold outside. A layer of fat around organs, such as our kidneys, helps protect these organs from injury. Fat is also an essential component of the walls of the body's millions of tiny cells and of the sheaths which cover the body's nerves.

As you can see dietary fats are essential. The problems arise when we have too many of them, especially the saturated variety and cholesterol. We shall look at the reasons for this in the next chapter.

CHAPTER 4

Health Benefits of the 3D Diet

As we saw in the previous chapter cholesterol is a fatty substance which is present in everyone's blood.

Now if cholesterol stayed in the blood there would be no problem. The trouble is that it doesn't. It has a fondness for the lining of the arteries through which blood passes and it becomes deposited in the lining, causing narrowing of the arteries.

Cholesterol is also an important constituent of atheromatous plaques. These are lumpy deposits on the inner lining surfaces of arteries. Plaques cause narrowing and blockage of the arteries. If the arteries to the heart are narrowed, not enough blood reaches the heart muscle during exertion and the resulting lack of oxygen causes a pain in the chest known as *angina pectoris*. If a coronary artery becomes severely narrowed it may be completely blocked. When this happens no blood can reach that part of the heart supplied by the affected artery and part of the heart muscle is destroyed. This is known as a *coronary thrombosis* or 'heart attack'.

The death rate from coronary heart disease has risen sharply in the past thirty years. In middle-aged (age 35 to 64) men coronary heart disease caused 20 per cent of deaths in 1951. This figure rose to an alarming 40 per cent in the 1970s. The death rate from coronary heart disease and arterial disease is higher in Scotland and Northern Ireland than anywhere else in the world, and the figures are almost as bad for England and Wales. About 170,000 people die from these diseases each year in the United Kingdom. Similar death rates from coronary heart disease are found elsewhere in the Western world including the United States.

Coronary heart disease is now the single commonest cause of death in middle age.

Why these atheromatous plaques form is still the subject of research, but there are at least six important factors. These are smoking, overweight, stress, lack of exercise, high blood pressure, and a high blood cholesterol.

People whose diet contains a good deal of saturated fatty acids and cholesterol tend to have high levels of cholesterol in their blood. People with high blood cholesterol levels have about double the risk of dying from coronary heart disease compared with that of people with normal cholesterol levels. People with coronary heart disease often have high colesterol levels. In Japan blood cholesterol levels tend to be low. But Japanese who move to San Francisco develop high cholesterol levels and an increased prevalence of coronary heart disease of a similar order to the native population.

THE OPINIONS OF THE WORLD'S EXPERTS

* *The American Heart Association* recommends that not more than half of our dietary fat (which currently forms about 38 per cent of our total calorie intake) should be saturated fats, and that the total consumption of fats should be reduced.

* *The Department of Health in the United Kingdom* published a report *Diet and Coronary Heart Disease* in 1974 in which it recommended the reduction of the consumption of saturated fats.

* *The Royal College of Physicians of London* and the *British Cardiac Society* in their 1976 report *The Prevention of Coronary Heart Disease* made the same recommendation.

* *The Lancet* reported in 1981 the results of the *Oslo Heart Study*. This described the favourable results in regard to the incidence and death rate from coronary heart disease in middle-aged men followed a reduced intake of saturated fat and cholesterol.

* The *World Health Organization* recommended in 1981 that saturated fats should represent not more than 10 per cent of

our total calorie intake, and it also stressed the importance of avoiding or correcting overweight.

* The authoritative *American Journal of Clinical Nutrition* reviewed in 1982 the results of the Framingham study, a large ongoing prospective study on the population of Framingham, USA, which is looking into various health risk factors such as smoking, high blood pressure and overweight. The study showed that the risk to a middle-aged man of acquiring coronary heart disease is directly related to his blood cholesterol level. The Journal concluded that a change in diet was needed, particularly the reduction of saturated fats and cholesterol.

So there is a consensus of medical opinion which is:

A diet low in saturated fats and cholesterol significantly reduces your risk of dying from coronary heart disease.

In addition to the undisputed connection between cholesterol and coronary heart disease there is now increasing evidence that a diet low in fats, especially saturated fats, reduces the risk of some cancers, especially of the bowel and the breast.

BUT WHAT IS THE RELEVANCE OF THE 3D DIET TO SLIMMING?

Fat is a highly concentrated source of calories. It contains about nine calories a gram (or about 260 calories an ounce). You can appreciate how brimming with calories fat is when you consider that carbohydrate – a popular target for many slimming diets – has only four calories a gram (or 115 calories an ounce). Protein has the same number of calories as carbohydrate. Even alcohol, which is generally regarded as being very fattening, has less calories than fat – about seven calories a gram (or about 200 calories an ounce). So if you reduce the amount of saturated fat in your diet you will reduce the amount of calories you consume. Saturated fats are, to a greater or lesser extent, replaced by carbohydrates and proteins, so that on the 3D Diet you do not necessarily eat less and therefore you do not become hungry. In fact it is quite possible actually to eat *more* food even though the calories are less.

It is not difficult to see why the 3D Diet has such a wide appeal. Slimming without necessarily having to reduce the amount of food you eat is an attractive idea. At the same time the diet enables you to do something positive about not one, but two, important risk factors to health and well-being – obesity and cholesterol.

CHAPTER 5

Lifestyle

WHY DO I WANT TO LOSE WEIGHT?

This is a question all slimmers ask themselves. The answer is likely to be one or both of these: first, to look more attractive; and second, to improve fitness. In this chapter we shall look at the second of these reasons.

I WANT TO BE FIT

Fitness is complete physical, mental and social well-being – *plus* good reserves of vital bodily functions – those of the heart, blood vessels, lungs and muscles – *plus* the absence of risk factors.

Whether or not we are fit depends partly on factors outside our control (such as congenital illness, inherited disease, many infections) and factors which we *can* control (such as smoking and overweight). How many of this second group of factors, which can result in *preventable* disease, apply in our lives depends on our *lifestyle.*

A healthy lifestyle is one in which risk factors are reduced to a minimum.

WHAT ARE THESE RISK FACTORS THAT CAN BE AVOIDED?

They are:
* cigarette smoking
* excess alcohol
* stress

* lack of exercise
* overweight
* incorrect diet

The last two in the above list are discussed elsewhere in this book.

SMOKING

Smoking causes disease and kills: this is a fact, not a matter of debate. If you smoke, you are 20 to 30 times more likely to die of lung disease – chronic bronchitis, emphysema, or lung cancer – than a non-smoker. You are about three times more likely to die of coronary heart disease than a non-smoker: and when you bear in mind that coronary heart disease is the single most common cause of death in middle age this is an alarming statistic. You are also more likely to suffer a stroke or to acquire one of a host of other diseases such as a peptic ulcer or cancer of the mouth, larynx, gullet or bladder.

ALCOHOL

First, the bad news: too much alcohol damages your health, in particular your liver, your weight, and your mental health. Second, the goods news: *in moderation* alcohol may be beneficial, for coronary heart disease is less common in people who have one or two drinks a day than those who never drink. But remember that the emphasis is on the word 'moderation'. The regular daily consumption of more than 60 grams of alcohol (about three pints of beer or three double measures of spirits or six glasses of wine) is a serious health hazard for men. Women are unfortunate in having metabolisms that have difficulty in coping with alcohol and their safe limits are about one-third of those for men – evolutionary sex discrimination!

STRESS

Stress is important in our lives as a motivating force. The

problems only arise if there is too much stress for us to cope with or if our mental constitution is so weakened that we cannot tolerate normal levels of stress, either of which situation may be looked upon as *overstress*. Overstress is harmful to health and causes a variety of conditions from nervous disease (anxiety, depression, 'nervous breakdowns') to heart attacks. There are many ways of dealing with overstress. Some are to do with easing pressures at work and perhaps setting more modest and realistic goals. Others depend on using a relaxation technique such as yoga, meditation, autogenics and self-hypnosis.

LACK OF EXERCISE

Most people inevitably think of exercise as a good way of controlling their weight. In fact exercise is not as efficient a way of losing weight as eating less food. For example if you walk one mile at a moderate place you will burn up the same number of calories as there are in a slice of bread or a cream cracker or an ounce of plain chocolate. But don't let that depress you because in addition exercise increases your body's metabolic rate which helps to burn up more of the calories that you have eaten.

The main benefit of exercise is that it increases your general level of fitness and probably helps to prevent coronary heart disease, which is commoner in overweight people than in others.

How much exercise should I take?
This depends on how overweight you are. If you are very overweight you should consult your doctor first, and he may suggest that you should take only very mild exercise until you have lost some weight. But if you are only moderately overweight and your general health is good there is no reason why you should not embark on gentle exercise, gradually increasing in the degree of exertion over a period of weeks. The important point is to avoid sudden or violent exertion which could cause muscular strain or even a

coronary thrombosis, either of which will immobilize you with the result that your weight problem will become even worse!

What sort of exercise should I take?
There are endless ways of exercising, but whichever you choose *regularity* is vital. A good brisk walk of 20 to 30 minutes three times a week is far better than a run of an hour or more or a game of squash just once a week. New, unaccustomed activities, especially if they are vigorous, can be dangerous and it is generally better to extend existing activities at least at first. Try to get into the habit of walking faster using stairs instead of lifts, and walking to the corner shop instead of using the car.

Planned programmes of exercise such as gym 'work-outs', the currently popular aerobics, or jogging, should be done only if you are sure that you are in good health and only if you enjoy doing them, otherwise you are unlikely to keep them up with any regularity. Whatever you do make sure that you break yourself in gently if you are not used to physical activity. Never let yourself become more than *mildly* breathless, and if you experience pain in your chest or if you have a heart condition consult your doctor.

Should I exercise before or after a meal?
Exercise after, rather than before, a meal leads to more food being oxidized to produce heat, and less food is changed into fat which is deposited in the body. So the answer is, exercise *after* a meal is better (but not in the first 45 minutes whilst your food is being digested).

A NEW FITTER YOU

A healthy lifestyle will make you fitter. If you are fitter you will be more strongly motivated to losing weight. At the same time losing weight will make you fitter.

You can now look forward to success because this book will show you how to achieve these three goals:
* *You will eat healthily and enjoyably*

* *You will become fitter*
* *You will lose weight*

THE 3D DIET WORKS BECAUSE IT IS

* suitable for ALL the family
* easy to follow anywhere, not just at home
  and
* approved by world health experts.

TABLE: *Calorific values of popular activities*

Activity	Calories per minute
sitting or sleeping	1
badminton (singles)	7
cycling (10 mph)	8
dancing	5
gardening (light)	4
gardening (heavy digging)	8
golf	5
jogging	10
running	14
skipping (rope)	10
squash	10
swimming (33 yds/min)	7
table-tennis	5
tennis (singles)	7
walking (2 mph)	3
walking (3 mph)	4.5
walking (4 mph)	6
walking (upstairs)	20
walking (downstairs)	8

CHAPTER 6

Fat Children

Fat children become fat adults. If you are a parent there is a lot that you can do to help your child.

Overweight children are usually very unhappy but often will not admit it. It is sad to see so many small children who are really podgy. Their parents are doing them a disservice that will affect them for the rest of their lives. Most healthy children are so active that their calorie intake can be enormous before they become fat. Unfortunately fat children very often start by being fat babies and so always lead restricted lives in terms of exercise and general wellbeing. So let us start right at the beginning.

DON'T LET THE PROBLEM ARISE

BABIES

So often how much a baby eats and weighs turns into a competition with baby Johnny down the road. So instead of allowing baby to stop when he has finished sucking either at the breast or the bottle he is actively encouraged to have a little more. Each extra half-an-ounce is seen as a triumph by the mother. But a baby does *not* need to finish every drop of every bottle or to suck to the last second of the allotted breastfeed time.

Another common mistake with small babies is offering a milk feed everytime the baby cries. Many mums fail to realize that a baby will often cry because he is thirsty and what he needs is a drink. Do follow advice given at your baby clinic, and if you are not sure which foods to give your baby do not be afraid to ask.

29

TODDLERS AND SMALL CHILDREN

Try not to get into the habit of giving toddlers and children sweets and biscuits on a daily basis, and *never* offer these as a reward for being good. Start good habits of a lifetime by encouraging children to eat fruit rather than crisps and 'junk' food everytime they feel hungry. This can be difficult because of the persuasive influence of television and magazines and other children, but it is worthwhile being firm but gentle.

Your children's reward will be good teeth, trim bodies and bags of energy.

Almost all children are vain to a certain extent, and the promise of an attractive body and pearly white teeth without fillings often adds weight to your argument. Also you can wage your own personal war against the media. For instance, in our house, in answer to one TV commercial for a well known highly calorific chocolate caramel bar our children sing their own words along with the commercial: 'A . . . a day helps your teeth rot away!'

Toddlers and small children very often *seem* to eat very little. But so long as they are healthy then there is no need to worry about their food consumption. The important point is to make sure that they do not binge between meals on chocolate biscuits, sweets, and so on. It is amazing how often a mother will say that her child never eats at mealtimes. But then when you spend some time with the child it soon becomes apparent that the child is eating all the time *except* at mealtimes. Crisps here, sweets there, biscuits here, and so on.

BUT WHAT DO YOU DO WITH A CHILD WHO IS ALREADY FAT?

Once a child becomes fat it is much more difficult to slim him down than it is to prevent the problem from arising in the first place. However, if your problem is that you already have a fat child (and remember that 'puppy' fat is just the same as any other kind of fat!) there is no need to despair. If you follow the basic methods of food preparation in this book you will be helping your child to eat more healthily. The principles of sensible eating are the same whether you are an adult or a child. The only difference is that an overweight adult aims to lose weight, whereas an overweight child should maintain the same weight as he continues to grow.

Many children love burgers, chips, fish fingers, and so on – 'forbidden' foods in most people's minds. In fact there is no reason at all why children may not eat them providing this is done sensibly. For example, if possible, grill these foods rather than fry them. Substitute jacket potatoes for chips. Don't fill children up with enormous portions of fattening commercially-produced puddings. Give ice cream addicts small portions topped with slices of fresh fruit. Don't say no and have an irritable child. Try instead to use your imagination and the ideas in this book to keep you and your offspring happy.

We think that there is little point in giving a separate section of recipes for children in this book because, by and large, children should eat much the same as adults. Instead here is an example of a week's menus for children to provide them with nourishing teatime meals when they come home from school.

Monday	grilled beefburger (100 per cent beef-type) with jacket potato and spaghetti hoops *followed by* banana and custard
Tuesday	3 fish fingers with baked beans and a slice of wholemeal bread and St Ivel Gold margarine *followed by* a *small* portion of ice cream served with chopped apple
Wednesday	1 *lean* pork chop, sprinkled with a little sage and onion stuffing, baked in the oven, gas

mark 6, 400°F (200°C), for 40 minutes, and
served with mashed potatoes and carrots
followed by 1 fruit yoghurt.

Thursday   Chicken Maryland (see recipe on page 72)
followed by fruit jelly with a *small* portion of ice
cream

Friday   Ham or other cold meat (with the visible fat
removed) with a *small* portion of chips and
salad (see pages 93 to 102 for ideas)
followed by baked apple and custard

Of course the size of the portion cannot be laid down as
this depends on many factors, such as the age of the child,
whether or not the child is already overweight and, if so, by
how much. If the child is not overweight then his appetite is
a good guide. Some children are blessed with efficient
metabolisms which burn up *all* the calories that they
consume in excess of their bodies' requirements. If such a
child has an enormous appetite there is nothing to worry
about so long as his food is nutritionally sound. Of our own
two children one is daily 'dying of terminal starvation' at
the end of each schoolday. Sometimes her meal is not ready
for when she is about to expire, and so there is always ready
a plate of low calorie foods that she likes, which will stop her
from raiding the biscuit tin. Typical foods are a chopped-up
carrot, a thinly sliced cucumber, radishes, a green pepper, a
slice of melon, or orange slices. These invariably shut her up
and keep her happy whilst her main feeding bag is being
prepared.

If you experiment with various foods it is possible to find
alternatives to an excess of sticky and sickly sweet things.
There are many excellent books on food for babies and
children, and if you are really stuck do consult them.
Remember, though, that the same basic rules apply to
overweight children as to overweight adults: too much of

the wrong kinds of food is what makes people fat. Very often a child's overweight starts in babyhood with an over-anxious Mum and continues through to the teenage years when there may develop very unhealthy and unwanted worries about weight which in turn perpetuate bad eating habits that may last a lifetime. Children brought up with good eating habits all through their childhood will have received a cheap but very precious gift that will last them the rest of their lives. It really costs only the time that it takes you to put some thought into what they are eating, and this can even save money on costly chocolate bars, sweets, crisps, not to mention expensive dental bills later.

DON'T SAY NO TO EVERYTHING!

Unless your child is overweight do not try to ban anything totally as this tends to result in food cravings. The calories from the occasional doughnut or packet of crisps will be quickly burned up by a child of average weight. If your child is overweight it is important to compensate for 'forbidden' foods with low calorie foods as suggested in the recipes described in this book. Remember that a large bowl of filling and comforting but low calorie soup can be very helpful as can puddings prepared in a low calorie, low saturated fats manner.

SCHOOL MEALS

There are many schools, even today, which provide stodgy fattening food at lunchtime. It still seems to be a popular idea in such places that it is a virtue for children to eat enormous portions and that it is even more virtuous to have second and even third helpings. You may be unlucky enough to recognize this in your children's school and you may have noticed that your children put on weight during term and that they shed the weight easily during the holiday. If this is so then do campaign at the school for a more sensible and enlightened approach. It may have been sensible long ago in unheated schools, full of undernourished children, to provide highly calorific food. But today there is a far higher percentage of overweight children, and there are very few children who are undernourished.

Of course, some children may be poorly fed in terms of a well balanced diet but certainly not in terms of calorie intake. Most schools would save time, money and effort if they cut out the pudding course three days a week and replaced it with fresh fruit, such as an apple or a fruit yoghurt. If your children go to a school where either they do not like the food or you know that the diet is poorly balanced take advantage of the option (if available) of providing packed lunches. Even a humble sandwich, thoughtfully prepared with good bread and fillings, can be very nutritious (see section in this book on snacks and sandwiches).

DOTING GRANDPARENTS

A quick word at this point to grandparents. Your grand-children will still love you – later on even more – if their treat when they see you is not always a packet of sweets but, perhaps, pennies to be added to their holiday savings. In summer why not a delicious peach? Even a comic is preferable to sweets every visit.

Finally, in this chapter, a word of caution. It is not our intention to bring up a nation of potential anorectics. Please do not nag your children (unless they are ill because of their excess weight), but very subtly and gently try to alter their eating habits without them even realizing it. We do not want children who are going through a slightly podgy stage to be made to feel freaky or uncomfortable. Rather they should be guided along sensible lines.

Do remember, too, that we are all different shapes. Do not expect everyone to have a Twiggy-like shape, even in childhood. Bone structure dictates the shape of your child's body, and even quite young girls can have fairly pronounced hips without having a weight problem.

34

CHAPTER 7

Eating Hints

Look at animals who live in the wild and you will almost certainly never find a fat one. This is because animals who have to hunt and kill their food do so only when they are hungry. And having eaten they stop as soon as they no longer feel hungry even if there is still food left. A breastfed baby will suck only when he is hungry, and he stops as soon as he has had enough. It is only when he is put on the bottle that his mother feels that the amount of milk she can see in the bottle is the amount of food he needs, and he is pressured into eating more than he really wants. As the baby grows up he is conditioned into believing that there is something very wrong about leaving food on the plate. As an adult he feels it is discourteous, even rude, not to eat everything that is put in front of him. Add to this boredom, anger, depression, or just sheer habit, and you have a collection of typical reasons for overeating.

So, apart from a diet, it is important to think very carefully about not only *what* we eat but *why* we eat it, and when and where. We can take a tip from the *gourmet* who enjoys his food not for its quantity but for its taste, its smell, its texture. He does not gulp his wine: he sips it slowly, savouring every drop. He eats *slowly*, chewing each mouthful of food thoughtfully, lovingly.

The following hints will help you to eat like a gourmet.

Remember, this means eating less but at the same time ENJOY-ING your food.

SHOPPING

* *Shop for food as soon as possible after a meal rather than when your stomach is empty.* You are likely to buy less food then because you are not hungry.
* *Make a list of the foods you intend to buy. Keep that list in your hand whilst shopping and stick rigidly to it.* Then you will be less likely to be tempted by colourful and attractive foods you had not intended to buy.
* *Limit the amount of money you take with you to that which you will need for the food on your list and no more.* This is for the same reason as the previous hint.
* *List the shops at which you intend to buy food and do not enter other food shops.* This hint was suggested to me by one of my patients who could never walk past a food shop without going in and buying some.

MEAL PLANNING

* *Avoid excessive hunger by having regular planned meals. Plan these meals daily and stick to them.* The person who has only a cup of coffee for breakfast and no lunch is likely to be so hungry by the evening that he eats more food in his evening meal than he might have done if he had eaten three meals (when his total calorie intake would probably have been less than that in one meal a day). Skipped meals tend to cause excessive hunger, and this leads to gorging.
* *Eat only if and when you are hungry. If you are not hungry DO NOT EAT.* It is amazing how much food most of us eat when we are not in fact hungry.
* *Do not overdraw on your calories in advance.* It is tempting to have a mid-morning snack and say to yourself that you will go without your lunchtime pudding to make up for it. Unfortunately it is likely that by the time lunchtime arrives you will still have your pudding!

THE MEAL ITSELF

* *When eating at home eat all your meals in one room in the house only*. Look upon eating as an 'activity' with its own time and *place* as you would any other activity. For example, you wash in a bathroom. You sleep in a bedroom. You swim in a swimming pool. You drive a car on a road. In the same way, whenever you eat at home, you should eat in your 'eating room', which is *one* room and one room only - usually either the dining room or the breakfast room *or* the kitchen.

* *Always eat in the same place in the one room in which you have your meals*. Make this space in your home your personal 'eating area'.

* *Eat only when you are sitting at a dining table*.

* *Never put anything in your mouth (except a toothbrush) whilst you are standing*.

* *While eating, periodically ask yourself, 'Am I still hungry?' If your honest answer is no, stop eating*. This is a very, very useful hint. Hunger is the cue to eat: lack of hunger, or its disappearance or satisfaction, is the cue to stop eating. It goes against the grain to leave food on the plate. Most of us have been brought up to believe that it is wrong or ill-mannered to leave food on the plate. And yet the Royal Family, who probably have more social dining than almost everyone else, and who always exercise the utmost tact and diplomacy, follow this hint very strictly. Most of them eat only two or three mouthfuls of each of perhaps five or six courses, the rest of the food being left on the plates. They 'pace the meal' so that enough hunger is left for each succeeding course. In this way *every* course, including the pudding, can be tasted and enjoyed. A variation on this hint is to draw a line with your knife down the middle of every plateful of solid food you are served. Then eat half of the food and let the other half be returned to the kitchen.

* *Allow no other activity to take place while you are eating*. Unless you are 100 per cent aware of whether or not you are hungry you are likely to eat food mindlessly. Reading at the table, watching television, doing a crossword puzzle are activities

which distract your mind and make it difficult for you to focus on your hunger. Chatting is okay but try to avoid serious discussions. An added bonus of this hint is that it increases your enjoyment of food.

* *Always use a knife, fork or spoon for ALL food.* If you put food into your mouth with your fingers this does not seem so much like eating, as witness anyone who demolishes a bowl of peanuts without thinking about what he is doing.

* *Limit the time you allow yourself for each meal.* So long as you do not gobble your food to make up for your reduced time you will eat less food.

* *Put down your knife and fork or spoon for a set period between mouthfuls.* The more quickly you eat the more you eat. People who never put down their knives and forks between mouthfuls but cut up and prepare their next mouthful whilst still chewing tend to eat more quickly and therefore eat more food. So try putting down your knife and fork between mouthfuls for, say, one or two minutes.

* *Cut up your food into as many small pieces as you can.* And:

* *Serve your food on to a small plate and spread the food evenly over the plate.* These two hints make your plate look as if there is more food on it than there actually is.

* *Serve yourself small measured quantities of food rather than helping yourself AD LIB.*

* *Do not keep serving dishes on the table while you eat.* These two hints encourage you to start off with small portions and to avoid the temptation to have further helpings after you have begun eating.

AND NOW FOR SOME DELAYING TACTICS:

* *Chew each mouthful for as long as possible.*
* *Count how many mouthfuls you eat in, say, two minutes. Reduce the number of mouthfuls so that you eat more slowly.*
* *Make sure that all the food from each mouthful is swallowed before you put any more food into your mouth.*

WHEN YOU HAVE FINISHED EATING

This is the dangerous time when it is very tempting to pick at food so long as it remains in front of you.

* *After finishing your meal dispose of any leftovers immediately.*
* *Leave the table as soon as you have finished eating. If you can, leave the table between courses.*

If you have children and they ask you for chocolates, sweets, nuts, and so on, tell them to get them for themselves (providing, of course, that they are old enough to do so). Try to avoid contact with foods that may tempt you.

* *Let OTHERS get their own chocolates, sweets, biscuits and so on, from the cupboard.* If you *do* have chocolates yourself then limit the number you have. Don't leave the box of chocolates open in front of you, otherwise it is likely that chocolates will disappear into your mouth before you realize it.

AND FINALLY

The slimmer's chief enemy is boredom. Boredom causes you to eat just for something to do. It is worth spending a little time analysing your life to see if boredom is a regular feature. At the end of the day do you slump into a chair with one hand on the television control and the other in a box of chocolates? Do you make for the kitchen to see what you can find to tempt you in the fridge? If so why not do something a little more *active*? Cut the grass, water the plants, go for a walk, take up tennis, write a letter (*mental* activity is as effective an antidote to boredom as the physical kind). So:

* *Adopt a positive attitude. Exchange calorie-burning activities for calorie-consuming ones. Modify your whole lifestyle to this end, and enjoy your life all the more.* If you do you are much more likely to end up fitter and slimmer, and you will probably enjoy life all the more.

CHAPTER 8

General Advice About the 3D Diet

Chapters 10-20 of this book gives specific advice about the 3D Diet through detailed recipes and menus. But because you will probably eventually want to devise your own meals it is useful to appreciate the principles of the diet which also serve as general recommendations.

The basis of the diet is twofold. First, alternative foods are swapped for foods containing a lot of saturated fats or cholesterol. Second, less calorific ways of preparing and consuming food and drink are used. (There will of course be some overlap between these two basic points.)

FOODS CONTAINING A LOT OF SATURATED FATS

(a) Fatty meats (beef, lamb and, in particular, pork), corned beef, luncheon meats, sausages, meat paste, pork pie, salami, duck, goose, and poultry skin. If and when you do eat meat make sure that you have very lean cuts and cut off the visible fat (each ounce cut off saving 260 calories). Avoid pre-minced beef which is usually very fatty.

SWAP ALTERNATIVES: *Chicken, turkey, veal, hare, rabbit, venison and game.*

(b) Whole milk (includes pasteurized, homogenized, condensed and evaporated).

SWAP ALTERNATIVE: *Skimmed milk.*

As well as helping to keep your blood cholesterol level low, using skimmed milk in place of whole milk saves 180 calories a pint.

(c) Whole milk products. These include:

(i) yoghurt.

SWAP ALTERNATIVE: *Low-fat natural yoghurt.*

An added bonus is that this saves 45 calories each 140g (5 ounce) portion. Remember that fruit yoghurts contain sugar and are very fattening.

(ii) butter and ordinary margarines.

SWAP ALTERNATIVES: *Low-fat margarine, eg St Ivel Gold. For cooking: corn oil, sunflower oil, safflower oil, soya oil, or margarine containing at least 50 per cent polyunsaturated fatty acids, eg Flora.*

(iii) whole milk drinks (such as milk shakes and chocolate).

SWAP ALTERNATIVE: Once again use *Skimmed milk.*

(iv) non-dairy coffee creamers.

SWAP ALTERNATIVE: *Skimmed milk.*

(v) whole milk cheeses (such as cream cheese, Cheddar, Cheshire and Stilton).

SWAP ALTERNATIVES: *Low-fat cheeses (such as cottage cheese) and medium fat cheeses (such as Edam).* There is also a new range of low fat Cheddar and Cheshire type cheeses called Tendale.

A low-fat cheese, such as cottage cheese, saves 135 calories for each 45g (1½ ounce) portion compared with a full fat cheese, such as Cheddar. If you adore full fat cheeses then limit yourself to one ounce a week.

(d) Cakes, puddings and biscuits made with whole milk, fats or eggs. These include pancakes, suet puddings, waffles, pancakes, ice cream, doughnuts and most biscuits.

SWAP ALTERNATIVES: *Puddings made with skimmed milk (for example, custard and blancmange) or egg whites (meringues, for example) and jellies.*

A bonus is that the alternatives contain much less saturated fat and fewer calories. If sorbet is substituted for ice cream you can save more than 100 calories in a 55g (2 ounce) portion.

You should also cut down on or avoid:

(e) salad cream and mayonnaise (unless the mayonnaise is made with a polyunsaturated oil, eg the recipes on pages 125–6 or Flora Sunflower Dressing),

(f) vegetables prepared or cooked in saturated fats, examples being potato salad and potato crisps,

(g) vegetables tinned in sauces, such as baked beans,

(h) peanuts, cashew nuts, coconuts,

(i) chocolate, toffees, fudge, butterscotch, caramel.

FOODS CONTAINING A LOT OF CHOLESTEROL

(a) Cream.

SWAP ALTERNATIVES: *skimmed milk, low-fat natural yoghurt.*

A bonus in avoiding cream is that each 30g (1 ounce) whose temptation you resist will also save you 250 calories.

(b) Creamed soups.

SWAP ALTERNATIVES: *Consommes and home-made soups made with skimmed milk or low-fat natural yoghurt in place of cream.*

As well as having little or no cholesterol the alternatives are far less calorific.

(c) Certain seafoods. These include caviare and roe (and remember that roe is the main ingredient of the fish pâté, Taramasalata). Most shellfish, such as crab, lobster, shrimps and prawns, should be avoided too.

SWAP ALTERNATIVES: *All other fish.*

You should also cut down on:

(d) Egg yolks. Limit yourself to three eggs a week. Don't forget that eggs are used in cooking, examples being cakes, omelettes and souffles.

(e) Offal, that is, liver, liver pâtés, kidney, sweetbread, brain and heart.

REDUCING CALORIES

There are four very useful tips:

1. *Cut out sugar*
Each teaspoon of sugar contains 25 calories and otherwise

42

has no nutritional value at all. If you have a 'sweet tooth' either train your taste buds away from sweetness or else use artificial sweeteners such as saccharine. The first alternative is the better one because you will find yourself less tempted by a whole variety of sweet and fattening foods – cakes, biscuits, sweet puddings, and so on. A good start is to reduce the amount of sugar that you put into your cups of tea and coffee. Try cutting down by one teaspoon – or even half a teaspoon – each week until you find yourself quite happy with no sugar at all.

If you find it impossible to cut out your desire for sweet tastes then switch to artificial sweeteners. As well as tablets these are available in liquid and powder forms which makes it easy to use artificial sweeteners on breakfast cereals or strawberries. They can also be used in cooking. Some people dislike their taste at first but it is surprising how quickly a taste for them can be acquired.

As well as obvious sugar all 'hidden' forms of sugar should be avoided. Syrup in tinned fruit is an example of this. Fortunately tinned fruit without the highly calorific syrup is now available.

Another example of hidden sugar are soft drinks. If you stick to low-calorie versions you will save at least 70 calories a glass. An added bonus is that some low-calorie drinks, particularly tonic water, are more appealing to some palates than drinks made with sugar. Here is a very useful slimming tip: when you feel tempted to put something in your mouth and it is not yet time for a meal pour yourself a low-calorie tonic water or lemonade. Make an occasion out of it by adding ice cubes, a slice of lemon, even some Angostura bitters. Sit down to drink it. Enjoy it, savour it, sip by delicious sip.

2. *If you can, develop a preference for wholemeal varieties of bread, pasta and rice, and choose high fibre breakfast cereals.*

Fibre has a filling effect. It also provides roughage which may be very useful when you are on a weight-reducing diet. Remember, too, that fresh fruit and vegetables are good sources of fibre without being too calorific.

3. *Use the least fattening method of preparing or cooking food.*

This will result in your consuming less saturated fats or fewer calories or both. As an example, a typical portion of grilled bacon saves 100 calories compared with the same portion of fried, and for most palates, tastes much better because it is less greasy. Fried foods should be avoided to a large extent, but on the odd occasion when the urge to eat something fried proves irresistible use a non-stick pan. This allows you to fry food in its own fat. An egg, for example, can be fried without added oil or butter, with a consequent saving of 40 calories. Vegetables can be pre-fried without oil or fat, so that if you are preparing a minced meat dish with vegetables first heat the meat slowly and then add the vegetables.

There are countless other calorie savings to be made, and you will find these well illustrated in the recipes in this book. For example, have you thought of using a single crust rather than a double crust on steak pies? Or have you ever stopped to think if it is really necessary to thicken your gravy with calorific flour? And when roasting meat place the meat on a rack in a roasting pan so that you can pour the fat away. Here are some other ways of reducing calories (some of which have already been mentioned in the sections above):

* Use skimmed milk instead of whole milk (*half* the calories).
* Use artificial sweeteners instead of sugar.
* Grill instead of fry.
* When roasting meat place it on a rack in the roasting tin so that the fat drains away. Do not use the pan dripping for making gravy, but use vegetable stock, a stock cube or gravy powder instead.
* Spread margarine, marmalade, jam, etc *thinly* over bread and toast.
* Don't use flour to thicken sauces (typically can save 50 calories).
* If you *must* use oil use as little as possible. For example, when browning meat use one *teaspoon* of oil rather than the more usual *tablespoon* – quite possible if you take care and use

44

a heavy-based casserole, and you may save as much as 90 calories.

* Use low-fat natural yoghurt instead of cream whenever possible (you will find countless examples of this in the recipes in this book). This can save hundreds of calories.

4. *Drink alcohol in moderation.*

It is amazing how often people overlook alcoholic drinks in their calculations of their daily calorie intake. Yet alcohol is not much less fattening than fat since it contains seven calories a gram. A typical drink, such as half a pint of a light beer, a glass of wine, a single sherry or a single measure of spirits, typically contains between 65 and 90 calories. And if you add an ordinary (as opposed to a low-calorie) mixer to your gin or whisky you may well double that figure.

However, please note that we have said drink alcohol in moderation, *not* cut it out altogether. As mentioned in the previous chapter moderate amounts of alcohol may actually be beneficial.

CHAPTER 9

Your Slimming Plan

The 3D Diet is a 'free' diet. This means that you are free to choose what you eat each day, providing you stick mainly to certain foods and you avoid other foods. You will see from the recipes in Chapters 10-20 of this book that the range of foods that you can choose from is very wide indeed.

Step 1

Decide on your target weight. The tables on pages 166 to 170 will help you *but do please read the footnote after the tables*.

Step 2

Decide how many calories you are allowed each day. Look at the following table:

	pts		pts
male	2	female	1
very active	2	sedentary	1
strong appetite	2	poor appetite	1
starting to slim	2	already dieting	1
each stone or part of a stone overweight			
(up to 3 stones)			1

For example, if you are male, 2 stones 4 pounds overweight, very active, with a strong appetite and you haven't yet started to diet you would score these points:

male	2
very active	2
strong appetite	2
starting to slim	2
2 stones 4 pounds overweight	3
Total:	11

But if you are female, 12 pounds overweight, fairly inactive, with a poor appetite, and already on a diet you would score:

female	1
inactive	1
poor appetite	1
already on a diet	1
12 pounds overweight	1
Total:	5

Your daily calorie intake will be:

5 to 7 points:	1,000 calories
8 or 9 points:	1,250 calories
10 or 11 points:	1,500 calories

The reason for this system of points is straightforward. Men tend to lose weight more easily than women, and so they can allow themselves more calories each day. Clearly the more active you are the more calories you burn up, and therefore the more calories you can consume. If you have a strong appetite you will not be so happy on as low a calorie intake as someone with a poor appetite, and the flexibility of the 3D Diet takes this into account. If you are just starting to slim the excess weight tends to fall away more easily than if you have already been dieting and lost an appreciable amount of weight.

Step 3

Decide your daily limits of saturated fats and cholesterol

consumption. Experts, including the World Health Organization, recommend a reduction of total fat consumption and, in particular, a reduction of *saturated* fats to 10 per cent of the total calorie intake. Your daily intake of saturated fats is as follows:

Calories daily	saturated fats grams daily
1,000	11
1,250	14
1,500	17

Whatever your calorie intake your cholesterol should be limited to 300mg daily.

DAILY MENUS

The dietary aims of the menus are the control of your consumption of calories, saturated fats, and cholesterol.

Two points about the recipes. First, this is not a cookery book. It is intended mainly as a book of suggestions and ideas. Each recipe will have three sets of figures after it, such as:

Cal: 250   S: 10   C: 70

This means that the recipe described has approximately 250 calories, 10g of saturated fats and 70mg of cholesterol in each portion.

This may seem complicated. In reality it isn't. If you follow the recipes described in this book it is unlikely that you would exceed the recommended intakes of saturated fats and cholesterol even if you do not actually keep a careful count of them. In any event you will find that after a short time you will be 'thinking' low saturated fats and low cholesterol whenever you consider food. The right foods to eat and those which you should avoid will become second-nature.

48

Second, many recipes mention that you should season according to taste. Now, too much salt may cause an increase in blood pressure. So try to keep its quantity as low as you reasonably can. And add little or no salt to the food at the table.

HOW FAST WILL I LOSE WEIGHT?

Many slimmers are led to believe in and expect *rapid* weight loss. In fact, this is both misleading and counterproductive. It is misleading because much of the apparent weight loss (if it occurs rapidly) is water rather than fat; and rapid weight loss is counterproductive because lean tissue (such as muscle) is lost in addition to water and fat. Because your resting metabolic rate depends largely on the amount of lean tissue in your body, the loss of lean tissue results in the lowering of your body's metabolic rate. This makes slimming more difficult and if you ever subsequently regain weight (as inevitably seems to happen after rapid weight loss) that weight is in the form of fat which further lowers the metabolic rate.

Repeated rapid weight loss may actually lead to an INCREASE in your weight in the long term.

The ideal rate of weight loss is one kilogram (two pounds a week) after the first week (when a lot of water tends to be shed).

WHAT IF I DON'T LOSE WEIGHT AT THIS RATE?

Weight loss is not usually perfectly consistent. Many people find that they lose one or two pounds a week for a while and then they 'stick' at the same weight for some time, often several weeks. Such a 'plateau' is perfectly normal and if this happens to you don't be discouraged. And *don't* give up your diet. Stick with your diet and then when your body's metabolism has adjusted to your reduced weight you will find that your weight will start to come off again. These plateaus tend to occur more and more often the nearer that you get to your target weight.

Don't forget, too, that if you are a woman fluid retention just before each monthly period may result in a temporary gain in weight. But remember that it is only temporary and don't be discouraged.

Weigh yourself once or twice a week as soon as you get up in the morning. This is the time of day when your weight is most likely to be least affected by what you have eaten or drunk in the previous 24 hours.

CHAPTER 10

Breakfasts

Breakfast is the most important meal as it marks the start of a new day. Do not be tempted to skip it. Besides, by using skimmed milk, artificial sweeteners, low-fat spreads, and grilling instead of frying, you can keep the calories and saturated fat and cholesterol intake down quite easily. So it really is not worth trying to get through the morning with an unpleasantly empty tum.

Start with a fruit juice and use artificial sweeteners (if you have a sweet tooth, that is) and skimmed milk in your tea and coffee.

There are many quickly prepared basic ways of starting the day that are both tasty and healthy. In addition we will also give you a few ideas for days when you have more time for a leisurely breakfast or when you simply have the desire for something different.

Let us look first at basic breakfasts for going to work on, doing the housework, and so on. Incidentally powder or granulated artificial sweeteners are more convenient than liquid forms for use on cereals.

WEETABIX

1 Weetabix
55ml (2 oz) skimmed milk
granulated artificial sweetener

Sprinkle the sweetener to taste over the Weetabix and serve with hot or cold skimmed milk.

Serves 1   Cal: 80   S: ½   C: 1.

WEETABIX AND BRAN

1 Weetabix
15g (½ oz) bran
55ml (2 oz) skimmed milk
granulated artificial sweetener

Serve as in the previous breakfast, sprinkling the bran over
the Weetabix.

Serves 1   Cal: 80   S: ½   C: 1.

SHREDDED WHEAT

1 shredded wheat
55ml (2 oz) skimmed milk
granulated artificial sweetener

Sprinkle the sweetener to taste over the shredded wheat and
serve with hot or cold skimmed milk.

Serves 1   Cal: 110   S: ½   C: 1.

SHREDDED WHEAT WITH BRAN

1 shredded wheat
15g (½ oz) bran
55ml (2 oz) skimmed milk
granulated artificial sweetener

Serve as in the previous breakfast, sprinkling the bran over
the shredded wheat.

Serves 1   Cal: 110   S: ½   C: 1.

INSTANT PORRIDGE

30g (1 oz) Ready Brek
140ml (¼ pint) skimmed milk
granulated artificial sweetener

Sprinkle the sweetener to taste over the Ready Brek, mix
with hot or cold skimmed milk, and serve.

Serves 1   Cal: 165   S: ½   C: 3.

INSTANT PORRIDGE WITH BRAN

30g (1 oz) Ready Brek
15g (½ oz) bran
140ml (¼ pint) skimmed milk
granulated artificial sweetener

Serve as in the previous breakfast, sprinkling the bran over
the porridge.

Serves 4   Cal: 165   S: ½   C: 3.

MUESLI

30g (1 oz) Muesli
55ml (2 oz) skimmed milk
granulated artificial sweetener

Sprinkle the sweetener to taste over the Muesli and serve
with hot or cold skimmed milk.

Serves 1   Cal: 130   S: ½   C: 1.

MUESLI WITH BRAN

30g (1 oz) Muesli
15g (½) bran
55ml (2 oz) skimmed milk
granulated artificial sweetener

Serve as in the previous breakfast, sprinkling the bran over
the Muesli.

Serves 1   Cal: 130   S: ½   C: 1.

The over-sweetened branded Mueslis should be avoided.
Many unsweetened varieties are available in health food
shops, delicatessens and larger supermarkets. Or you could
make your own mixture to suit your taste. The following
recipe is an example.

HOME MADE MUESLI

55g (2 oz) porridge oats

285ml (½ pint) unsweetened orange juice or apple juice
55g (2 oz) dried fruit, eg sultanas
30g (1 oz) nuts, eg hazelnuts
2 apples (chopped but not peeled) or 1 small banana
140ml (¼ pint) skimmed milk

Pour the juice over the oats and leave overnight. In the morning stir in the dried fruit, crushed nuts and chopped apple or banana. Divide into four portions and serve with one-quarter of the milk on each portion. No added sweetener should be necessary as the fruit will provide a lot of natural sweetness.

Serves 4   Cal: 130   S: ½   C: 1.

ALL-BRAN

55g (2 oz) All-Bran
55ml (2 oz) skimmed milk
granulated artificial sweetener

Sprinkle the sweetener to taste over the All-Bran and serve with hot or cold skimmed milk.

Serves 1   Cal: 170   S: ½   C: 2.

For all those who want a basic breakfast but who do not like cereals there are endless combinations of delicious ways to start the day with toast. Do use wholemeal bread, bread with bran or any of the wide variety of wholesome breads now available, and ignore white plastic. It may take a little getting used to but the effort is well worthwhile in terms of both taste and health.

First, a brief word about what you spread on the toast. (Incidentally the subject of spreads is discussed separately in chapter 17, but it is worth repeating the salient points here.) Remember that on this diet you are watching not only your calories but also saturated fats and cholesterol intake. Butter should therefore be avoided. There is a choice of two margarines. Flora is made entirely from vegetable oils and is high in polyunsaturated fats. St Ivel Gold is made from vegetable oils and buttermilk (similar to skimmed milk), but contains only half the amount of fat of Flora, and is therefore less calorific. We prefer the taste of St Ivel Gold on toast, but the choice is a personal one. Whichever you choose the important point is to spread the margarine *thinly*. The same applies to marmalade, and there is no reason at all why you should not enjoy the many superb varieties available, providing you spread it *thinly*.

TOAST AND MARMALADE

1 slice of wholemeal bread
7.5g (¼ oz) St Ivel Gold
5g (1 *level* tspn) marmalade

Toast the bread and spread with margarine and marmalade.

Serves 1   Cal: 100   S: ½   C: ½.

TOAST AND HONEY

1 slice of wholemeal bread
7.5g (¼ oz) St Ivel Gold
5g (1 *level* tspn) honey

Toast the bread and spread with margarine and honey.

Serves 1   Cal: 100   S: ½   C: ½.

TOAST AND MARMITE

1 slice of wholemeal bread
7.5 g (¼ oz) St Ivel Gold
Marmite to taste

Toast the bread and spread with margarine and Marmite.

Serves 1   Cal: 90   S: ½   C: 0.

TOAST AND GENTLEMAN'S RELISH

1 slice of wholemeal bread
7.5g (¼ oz) St Ivel Gold
Gentleman's Relish to taste

Toast the bread and spread with margarine and Gentleman's Relish.

Serves 1   Cal: 90   S: ½   C: ½.

TOAST AND PEANUT BUTTER

1 slice of wholemeal bread
15g (½ oz) peanut butter

Toast the bread and spread with peanut butter

Serves 1   Cal: 155   S: 3   C: ½.

For those cold mornings when you really would feel deprived if you did not have a 'cooked' breakfast there is no reason why you should not have one providing it is prepared in the least calorific way.

BACON ON TOAST

2 rashers lean back bacon
1 slice of wholemeal bread

Grill the bacon until it is crisp, and serve on the toasted bread.

Serves 1   Cal: 225   S: 1   C: 14.

Anyone not very familiar with grilling food will be amazed at the amount of fat (and therefore calories too) that is lost. This breakfast, for example, would take you nearly another 100 calories through your daily allowance if the bacon were fried rather than grilled. There really is no reason to fry foods such as bacon, sausages, burgers, and so on, as they all taste better and are healthier for you if grilled.

BACON AND BANANA

2 rashers lean back bacon
1 small banana

Grill the bacon until it is becoming crisp. Peel and slice

lengthwise the banana and grill it alongside the bacon for about two minutes. Serve together – a delicious combination.

Serves 1   Cal: 250   S: 1   C: 17.

SAUSAGE AND TOMATO

2 chipolatas
1 tomato
basil

Prick the sausages and grill. When they are almost cooked halve the tomato, sprinkle with basil, and place on the grill pan beside the sausages. Cook for about 5 minutes. Serve the sausages and tomato together.

Serves 1   Cal: 165   S: 4   C: 24.

MUSHROOMS AND TOMATO ON TOAST

4 medium mushrooms
1 tomato
1 slice of wholemeal bread
7.5g (¼ oz) Flora
basil

Slice the mushrooms and tomato and fry gently in the Flora for about 5 minutes. Meanwhile toast the bread. Serve the mushrooms and tomato very hot on the toast and sprinkle with basil.

Serves 1   Cal: 100   S: ½   C: ½.

COTTAGE CHEESE ON TOAST

1 slice of wholemeal bread
55g (2 oz) cottage cheese
7.5g (¼ oz) St Ivel Gold
freshly milled black pepper

Optional extra:
1 slice pineapple (fresh or canned in its own juice, but *not* canned in sweetened syrup)

Toast the bread, spread the margarine and cheese, and place grill until the cheese is slightly brown and bubbling. Serve hot, sprinkled with pepper, and topped with pineapple if available.

Serves 1   Cal: 135   S: 2   C: 7.

KIPPER AND LEMON

1 small kipper
½ lemon

Grill the kipper until cooked and serve with slices of lemon.

Serves 1   Cal: 90   S: 3   C: 65.

And now for really hungry mornings!

BEANS ON TOAST

1 140g (5 oz) tin baked beans
1 slice of wholemeal bread

Heat the beans and toast the bread. Spoon the beans over the toast and serve.

Serves 1   Cal: 155   S: ½   C: ½.

KEDGEREE

225g (8 oz) smoked haddock
115 (4 oz) cooked rice
1 slice lemon
salt
freshly milled black pepper

Cook the fish, then skin and flake it. Mix the fish with the rice, and season it with salt and pepper. Garnish the kedgeree with a slice of lemon.

Serves 2   Cal: 180   S: ½   C: 65.

Don't forget that warm sunny mornings can be started with wonderful fruity breakfasts.

MELON AND ORANGE WAKER

1 small melon
1 orange
4 slices wholemeal bread or rolls
30g (1 oz) St Ivel Gold for spreading

Slice the melon and cut it into cubes. Peel the orange and cut into slices. Place the melon cubes in 4 glass bowls and decorate with the orange slices. Serve with a slice of wholemeal bread or roll. Substitute an apple or small banana for the orange if you prefer.

Serves 4   Cal: 110   S: ½   C: ½.

APPLE AND PLUM COMPOTE

4 cooking apples
455g (1 lb) plums
4 slices wholemeal bread or rolls
30g (1 oz) St Ivel Gold for spreading
liquid or granulated artificial sweetener

The evening before gently stew the fruit together in a little water until soft, sweeten to taste, and place in the fridge overnight. Serve well chilled for a really refreshing start to the day with some wholemeal bread or rolls.

Serves 4   Cal: 190   S: ½   C: ½.

* Many of the recipes in this book mention that salt and pepper may be added to taste. As explained in chapter 8 it is wise to try to keep your intake of salt moderate. Try to add only a little salt in cooking and little or no salt to your food at the table.

* Many people find the idea of frying without oil daunting, and for this reason some of the recipes in this book mention *small* amounts of oil in the ingredients. However do try frying without any added oil. With practice and a good non-stick pan you will probably find this is quite easy to do, and you will have the bonus of further reducing your calorie intake.

CHAPTER 11

Soups and Other Starters

SOUPS

Home-made low-calorie soups are an enormous boon to slimmers because they can be very filling (and also very warming on a cold winter's day!).

LEEK AND POTATO SOUP

4 leeks
4 potatoes
2 onions
1140ml (2 pints) chicken stock
30g (1 oz) Flora
140ml (¼ pint) skimmed milk
salt and pepper

Peel and chop onions. Trim, slice and wash leeks. Melt margarine in heavy saucepan. Add sliced leeks and chopped onion, and fry gently for about 10 minutes. Add peeled and diced potatoes and cook for a further 5 minutes. Add chicken stock, salt and pepper, bring to the boil and simmer for 40 minutes. Liquidise the soup, return to saucepan, adding skimmed milk. Reheat and serve hot.

This soup may be served very cold.

Serves 6   Cal: 125   S: 1   C: ½.

CARROT AND ONION SOUP

2 onions
455g (1 lb) carrots
1 clove garlic

850ml (1½ pints) beef stock
30g (1 oz) Flora
30ml (2 tbspns) low-fat natural yoghurt
salt and pepper

Peel and thinly slice carrots. Skin and chop onion. Skin and crush garlic. Melt margarine in a large saucepan. Fry vegetables and garlic for 5 minutes. Add beef stock, salt and pepper. Bring to the boil and simmer for 20 minutes. Liquidise the soup. Reheat in a saucepan. Stir in yoghurt before serving.

Serves 4   Cal: 85   S: 1   C: ½.

CREAM OF MUSHROOM SOUP

1 small onion
225g (8 oz) mushrooms
55g (2 oz) flour
55g (2 oz) Flora
570ml (1 pint) chicken stock
570ml (1 pint) skimmed milk
salt and pepper

Skin and finely chop onion. Chop mushrooms. Cook onion in melted Flora in a saucepan. Fry till soft, then add chopped mushrooms and fry for 5 minutes. Add flour and stir well. Slowly add stock and milk to the mixture, stirring all the time. Add salt and pepper. Bring to the boil and simmer for 5 minutes.

Serves 4   Cal: 135   S: 3   C: 3.

TOMATO SOUP

1 large onion
1 clove garlic
680g (1½ lbs) tomatoes
1140ml (2 pints) chicken stock
30g (1 oz) Flora
5g (1 level tspn) sugar

2.5g (½ level tspn) dried basil
30ml (2 tbspns) low-fat natural yoghurt
salt and pepper

Skin and chop onion. Skin and crush garlic. Skin and chop
tomatoes (the easy way to skin tomatoes is to pour boiling
water over them in a bowl and leave for about a minute).
Melt margarine in a large saucepan. Gently fry onion and
garlic for 5 minutes. Add tomatoes and cook for about 2
minutes. Stir in stock, sugar, basil, salt and pepper. Bring to
the boil and simmer for 30 minutes. Liquidise the soup.
Reheat in a saucepan and stir in yoghurt.

Serves 6   Cal: 55   S: 1   C: ½.

CELERY SOUP

1 head of celery
30ml (2 tbspns) low-fat natural yoghurt
30g (1 oz) Flora
2 beef or chicken stock cubes
570ml (1 pint) water

Wash celery and chop into small pieces. Lightly fry the
celery for 5 minutes in the Flora in a saucepan. Dissolve
stock cubes in hot water. Pour over the celery and cook until
tender (about 30 minutes). Liquidise, return to pan, and stir
in the yoghurt. Season if necessary.

Serves 2   Cal: 115   S: 3   C: 1.

BORTSCH

1 large onion
1 large raw beetroot
1140ml (2 pints) stock
1 bay leaf
30ml (2 tbspns) low-fat natural yoghurt
30g (1 oz) Flora
parsley

Skin and slice the onion. Peel and cut the beetroot into

matchstick-size pieces. Melt the Flora in a saucepan and fry the onion for 5 minutes. Add the beetroot to the onion with the stock and bay leaf. Bring to the boil and cook for 1 hour.

To serve stir a spoonful of yoghurt in to each portion. Sprinkle with chopped parsley if available, and serve very hot.

Serves 6   Cal: 45   S: 1   C: ½.

BASIC VEGETABLE SOUP

910g (2 lb) mix of chopped root vegetable (eg potatoes, carrots, turnip, etc) and leeks, celery and onions
30g (1 oz) Flora
1140ml (2 pints) stock

Any combination of vegetables can be used to make a satisfying and delicious soup. For example, if you adore carrots then add more carrots and no potatoes.

Chop all the vegetables to an even size. Fry gently in the Flora in a saucepan for 5 to 10 minutes, stirring. Add the stock, bring to the boil and cook gently for 45 minutes.

This soup can be served as a chunky soup or it can be liquidised for a smooth thick soup. Season as required.

Serves 6   Cal: 80   S: 1   C: ½.

FRENCH ONION SOUP

455g (1 lb) onions
15g (½ oz) Flora
2 cloves garlic (crushed)
850ml (1½ pints) beef stock
2.5g (½ tspn) low-calorie granulated sweetener
freshly milled black pepper
parsley

Heat the Flora in a large saucepan. Slice the onions and add to the margarine. Stir in the garlic, add the sweetener, and cook over a low heat for 15 minutes until the onions brown.

Pour on the stock, bring to the boil, cover and gently simmer for 30 minutes. Season to taste and sprinkle with parsley.

Serves 4   Cal: 50   S: ½   C: ½.

The next three soups are very substantial and delicious, and a large portion of each could constitute a main meal, particularly if served with a slice of wholemeal bread.

LENTIL SOUP

225g (8 oz) lentils
1 onion
2 carrots
225g (8 oz) tinned tomatoes
30g (1 oz) Flora
2 cloves garlic (crushed)
2 pints stock
parsley

We find that there is a bewildering array of lentils (there are literally dozens of varieties!) on the market. Therefore our advice is to follow the cooking instructions on the packet of lentils that you buy.

Skin and chop the onion. Peel and chop the carrots. Melt the Flora in a saucepan and fry the onion and carrots for 5 minutes. Add the remaining ingredients. Bring to the boil and simmer gently for about 1 hour (depending on the type of lentil).

This soup can be served as it is or else you can liquidise it if you prefer a smooth soup. Sprinkle with parsley and season to taste.

Incidentally lentils are an excellent source of good protein. Although they are relatively deficient in sulphur-containing amino-acids they are rich in another essential amino-acid, lysine, in which many cereals are deficient. For this reason a combination of lentils and cereal provides a complete protein that compares well with animal protein.

65

So it is a good idea to have a slice of wholemeal bread with this soup.

Serves 6   Cal: 155   S: 1   C: ½.

FISH SOUP

455g (1 lb) haddock fillets
1 onion
1 leek
1 medium-size potato
4 tomatoes
30g (1 oz) Flora
salt and pepper
mixed herbs (optional)
850ml (1½ pints) water
parsley

Skin and cut the fish into bite-size pieces. Wash and slice the leek. Skin and chop the onion. Skin and chop the tomatoes. Peel and slice the potato. Melt the Flora in a large saucepan and add the vegetables. Stir gently for 5 minutes, add the fish and season well with salt and pepper, adding a few mixed herbs if desired. Pour the water over the mixture and simmer for 30 minutes.

Sprinkle each serving with parsley. Eaten with slices of good fresh wholemeal bread this dish makes a satisfying, nutritious and tasty meal.

Serves 4   Cal: 200   S: 1   C: 65.

The last of our 'main dish' soups is a wholesome bowl of delicious minestrone, ideal to warm you up on a cold winter's day. The recipe below, although leaving out some of the ingredients of a classic minestrone (in order to keep the saturated fat and calorie content low) nevertheless makes a very acceptable alternative.

MINESTRONE SOUP

2 sticks celery
1 large carrot
1 medium-sized potato
1 onion
1 leek
¼ small cabbage
1 small tin Cannellini beans
1 small tin of tomatoes
1 clove garlic (crushed)
115g (4 oz) pasta (preferably whole-wheat), pasta shapes,
  broken spaghetti, macaroni, etc
1700ml (3 pints) beef stock
30g (1 oz) Flora
55g (2 oz) Edam cheese
15g (1 level tbspn) tomato puree
1 pinch dried herbs (mixed or basil)
salt and pepper

The vegetable ingredients can be varied to suit your taste. For example, if you loathe leeks but love celery, leave out the leek and add an extra stick of celery.

Prepare the vegetables and slice evenly. Melt the Flora in a large heavy saucepan, add the vegetables and gently stir for 10 minutes. Add the garlic, salt and pepper, and stir well. Add the tomato puree and herbs, and then stir in the stock and bring to the boil. Simmer gently with the lid on for 30 minutes. Add the strained and rinsed Cannellini beans and the pasta and cook for a further 15 to 20 minutes. (Incidentally, dried haricot beans can be used instead of Cannellini beans, but using tinned pre-cooked beans is quicker and easier.) Check the seasoning.

Serve with grated Edam cheese sprinkled over the top.

Serves 4   Cal: 180   S: 3   C: 9.

GRAPEFRUIT COCKTAIL

1 grapefruit
1 orange
10ml (2 tspns) low-calorie granulated sweetener
2 sprigs of mint

Cut the grapefruit in half, remove the segments, and place each skin in a bowl. Peel the orange and divide it into segments. Mix the segments of the two fruits together with the sweetener until the sweetener has dissolved. Place the fruit in the grapefruit skins and top with the sprigs of mint. Serve chilled.

Serves 2   Cal: 60   S: 0   C: 0.

Melon on its own makes an excellent low-calorie starter. But if you want to 'doll it up' try the following dish.

MELON SALAD

2 small melons
225g (8 oz) black grapes
2 tomatoes
4 sprigs of mint

Cut the grapes in half and remove the seeds. Skin the tomatoes and cut into quarters. Cut the melons in half and remove the seeds. Scoop out the flesh and cut into cubes. Mix together the melon, grapes and tomatoes. Divide the mixture between the melon shells. Serve garnished with a sprig of mint each.

Serves 4   Cal: 60   S: 0   C: 0.

GUACOMOLE WITH CRUDITES

2 ripe avocado pears
2 tomatoes
½ small onion

1 clove garlic (crushed)
2.5ml (½ tspn) Worcestershire sauce
30ml (2 tbspns) low-fat natural yoghurt
juice of a whole lemon
salt
freshly milled black pepper

Ingredients for the crudité:
4 carrots
4 sticks celery
½ cucumber
1 green pepper
1 red pepper

Skin and chop the tomatoes. Grate the onion. Halve the avocado pears, remove the stones, scoop out the flesh, and mash with the lemon juice. Add the onion, tomatoes, garlic, Worcestershire sauce and yoghurt. Mix until smooth and add salt and pepper to taste. Place in a serving dish.

Cut the vegetables into even matchstick-size pieces. Put the avocado mixture on a large plate and arrange the vegetables round it. The strips of vegetable are used to dip into the avocado mixture.

Serves 4   Cal: 100   S: 2   C: ½.

TOMATO SALAD

455g (1 lb) ripe tomatoes
1 large onion
30 ml (2 tbspns) lemon juice
15g (1 tbspn) chopped parsley
salt
freshly milled black pepper

Slice the tomatoes and place in four bowls. Slice the onions into rings and place on top of the tomatoes. Just before serving sprinkle with lemon juice, parsley, salt and pepper.

Serve with herbed French bread.

Serves 4   Cal: 20   S: 0   C: 0.

SMOKED MACKEREL PÂTÉ

225g (8 oz) smoked mackerel, skinned and boned
55g (2 oz) St Ivel Gold margarine
juice of 1 lemon
freshly milled black pepper

Flake the flesh of the mackerel and place in a liquidiser or
processor. Add the margarine and lemon juice. Process until
smooth. Place in a serving dish, cover with cling film and
chill.

Serve with slices of wholemeal toast and lemon wedges.

Serves 4   Cal: 140   S: 4   C: 45.

LEEKS A LA GRECQUE

340g (12 oz) leeks
3 tomatoes
1 clove garlic, crushed
15ml (1 tbspn) polyunsaturated oil
juice of ½ lemon
salt
freshly milled black pepper
chopped parsley to garnish

Wash the leeks and cut into 2 to 3 cm (one inch) lengths.
Skin and chop the tomatoes. Put the leeks, tomatoes and
other ingredients into a pan, and season to taste. Simmer
gently for 20 minutes, then allow to cool.

To serve transfer to a serving dish and serve cold
garnished with parsley.

Serves 4   Cal: 60   S: ½   C: 0.

CHAPTER 12

Chicken Main Courses

Chicken is a good friend to 3D Diet slimmers because it is relatively low in cholesterol and saturated fats and also in calories, especially when roasted, grilled or poached. It is a good food to experiment with to create new dishes.

Incidentally, chicken leg has more saturated fats and cholesterol than chicken breast. And chicken skin is extremely calorific, so do try to avoid eating it!

BASIC ROAST CHICKEN

1 chicken
Seasoning to taste

Place the chicken in a roasting dish in an oven, gas mark 5, 375°F (190°C), with a cooking time of 20 minutes for each pound plus an extra 20 minutes. When it is cooked remove the chicken from the oven, place it on a warm dish and allow it to rest for a further 20 minutes. This resting period is well worthwhile because it makes the bird much easier to carve.

Pour off the excess fat, if any, in the roasting tin and use the remaining juices to make a gravy according to your tastes.

Serve with vegetables according to your preference and calorie allowance.

Serves 4 to 6 depending on the size of the chicken.

Cal: 145   S: 1   C: 85 (assuming 115g (4 oz) each portion).

We find that roast chicken makes an extremely nutritious and delicious base for a meal which requires the minimum of preparation. We use the word *base* because you can add

71

all sorts of vegetables and sauces to it which can be varied for each individual depending on their tastes and calorific requirements. For example one person may find that there is room in his daily calorie allowance for roast potatoes, whereas another person may prefer to eat boiled potatoes and allow more calories for stuffing and cranberry sauce or a richer pudding. To be able to roast a chicken simply with no additional fat you need to start with a good quality chicken which can then be simply roasted in the oven on its own. This of course can be eaten hot (with your own choice of vegetables) or cold (with a salad).

CHICKEN SALAD

910g (2 lb) cooked chicken (skinned)
55g (2 oz) commercial or home-made (see recipe, page 125) mayonnaise
55ml (2 oz) low-fat natural yoghurt
¼ cucumber (chopped)
1 lettuce
2 spring onions (chopped)
15g (1 tbspn) chopped parsley
1 red apple (sliced)
55g (2 oz) green grapes
salt
finely milled black pepper

Slice the chicken into even-sized pieces and place in a bowl. Mix the mayonnaise and yoghurt together in another bowl, add the onions, cucumber and parsley, and stir well. Pour this sauce over the chicken and arrange the chicken on a bed of lettuce leaves. Decorate with grapes and apple and sprinkle salt and pepper to taste.

Serves 4   Cal: 205   S: 2   C: 90.

CHICKEN MARYLAND

4 chicken breasts
1 egg white

55g (2 oz) wholemeal breadcrumbs
4 bananas
55ml (4 tbspns) orange juice
salt
freshly milled black pepper

Skin the chicken breasts. Lightly beat the egg white and season with salt and pepper. Dip the chicken breasts in the egg white, then coat evenly with the breadcrumbs. Place the chicken breasts in a baking dish and bake in a pre-heated oven, gas mark 5, 375° (190°C), for 45 to 60 minutes. 15 minutes before the end of the cooking time peel the bananas and slice in half lengthwise. Dip the bananas in the orange juice and place around the chicken breasts in the oven.

Serve the chicken breasts and bananas with a jacket potato and sweetcorn if your calorie allowance permits. Alternatively serve with a salad.

Serves 4   Cal: 270   S: 3   C: 175.

CHICKEN IN WINE

As the recipe has been somewhat changed from the traditional *coq au vin* we will refrain from calling it thus.

4 chicken joints
12 button onions
170g (6 oz) mushrooms (sliced)
285ml (½ pint) red wine
15g (1 tbspn) cornflour
30g (1 oz) Flora
2 cloves garlic (crushed)
bouquet garni
salt
freshly milled black pepper
parsley

Melt the Flora in a frying pan and fry the chicken joints until they are golden. Remove from the pan and place in a large casserole dish. In the same frying pan gently soften the

73

onions which are then added to the chicken. Mix the wine and cornflour together and gradually add them to the juices in the frying pan. Bring to the boil, stirring all the time, and cook for two minutes. Add the garlic, salt, pepper and bouquet garni to the chicken mixture. Pour the wine and cornflower mixture over the chicken. Cover and bake in an oven, gas mark 4, 350°F (180°C), for 45 minutes. Then take the chicken out of the oven and add the mushrooms to it. Return to the oven for a further 15 minutes.

Sprinkle with chopped parsley, and serve with mashed potato, rice or a salad.

Serves 4   Cal: 270   S: 4   C: 175.

CHICKEN TANDOORI

4 chicken breasts
1 onion (finely chopped)
285ml (10 oz) low-fat natural yoghurt
10g (2 tspns) curry powder
2.5g (½ tspn) ground ginger
5g (1 tspn) paprika
1 clove garlic (crushed)
30ml (2 tbspns) lemon juice
rind of a lemon (finely grated)
salt

Remove the skin and bones from the chicken breasts. Pierce them all over with a skewer and place in a shallow dish. Mix together all the other ingredients and pour over the chicken, cover and place in a fridge for 24 hours. Take the chicken from the marinade and place in a roasting tin and pour over any remaining marinade. Place in a pre-heated oven, gas mark 3, 325°F (165°C), for 1½ hours.

Serve with rice or a salad.

Serves 4   Cal: 185   S: 2   C: 155.

LEMON CHICKEN

4 chicken breasts
30ml (2 tbspns) polyunsaturated oil
55ml (4 tbspns) fresh lemon juice
rind of one lemon (grated)
2 cloves garlic (crushed)
salt
freshly milled black pepper

Place the chicken breasts in a greased shallow baking dish.
Mix the lemon juice, rind, oil and garlic together. Lightly
sprinkle the chicken pieces with a little salt and pepper.
Pour the lemon mixture evenly over the chicken. Cover and
bake in an oven, gas mark 4, 350°F (180°C), for 45 minutes,
basting occasionally. Remove the cover and cook for a
further 15 minutes to allow the chicken to brown slightly.

Before serving remove the chicken skin and sprinkle with
chopped parsley. Serve with noodles, creamed potatoes or a
salad.

Serves 4   Cal: 210   S: 3   C: 155.

CHICKEN WITH ROSEMARY

4 chicken pieces
10g (2 tspns) dried rosemary (or fresh if you have it)
salt
freshly milled black pepper

Rub the rosemary, salt and pepper into the chicken. Wrap
the chicken pieces in foil and bake in an oven, gas mark 5,
375°F (190°C), for 1 hour.

Serve with jacket potatoes and green vegetables.

Serves 4   Cal: 145   S: 1   C: 85.

CHICKEN CASSEROLE

4 chicken pieces
455g (1 lb) carrots
455g (1 lb) leeks

2 medium potatoes
1 medium onion
2 cloves garlic (crushed)
2 sticks celery
570ml (1 pint) chicken stock
15ml (1 tbspn) polyunsaturated oil

Prepare the vegetables by peeling and slicing into even-sized pieces. Heat the oil in a large heavy casserole. Fry the chicken pieces until they are golden. Remove the chicken and place on a warm plate. Gently fry all the vegetables in the casserole for five minutes and add the garlic. Return the chicken to the casserole, placing them on top of the softened vegetables. Pour the chicken stock over the chicken and cook in the oven, gas mark 2, 300°F (150°C), for 2½ hours.

This dish needs no accompanying vegetables.

Serves 4   Cal: 265   S: 3   C: 175.

CHICKEN WITH RICE

455g (1 lb) cooked chicken
1 green pepper
4 sticks celery
1 medium onion
115g (4 oz) mushrooms (sliced)
170g (6 oz) rice
1 clove garlic (crushed)
30g (1 oz) Flora
salt
freshly milled black pepper

Dice the chicken and put on one side. Cook the rice as directed on the packet. Meanwhile slice the vegetables into even-sized pieces. Melt the Flora in a frying pan and fry the onion and garlic for three minutes. Add the green pepper and celery and cook for a further five minutes. Add the chicken, mushrooms, salt and pepper. Cover and cook gently for another five minutes. When the rice is cooked mix

the rice and chicken and vegetable mixture together.
Serve with a salad.

Serves 4   Cal: 255   S: 2   C: 85.

CHICKEN AND TOMATOES

4 chicken pieces (skinned)
1 medium tin of tomatoes
2 medium onions (sliced)
1 bay leaf
15ml (1 tbspn) polyunsaturated oil
1 tspn low-calorie granulated artificial sweetener
salt
freshly milled black pepper

Heat the oil in a large casserole dish, add the chicken and fry until golden-brown. Remove the chicken and place on a plate. Fry the onions gently for five minutes. Add the tomatoes and place the chicken in the mixture. Add the bay leaf, sweetener, salt and pepper. Cover and cook in the oven, gas mark 4, 350°F (180°C), for 1½ hours.

Serve with jacket potato and noodles or a salad.

Serves 4   Cal: 190   S: 3   C: 175.

CHAPTER 13

Meat Main Courses

ROAST MEATS

Roasted meats, without any added fats so beloved in many cookery books, are easy to cook and are an excellent way of preparing meat on the 3D Diet because some of the fat is lost during the cooking.

Roast beef, served with horseradish sauce and wholemeal Yorkshire pudding (see recipe at end of pudding section on page 112) is delicious.

When roasting lamb choose leg rather than shoulder as it is much leaner. Serve whenever possible with *fresh* mint sauce.

ROAST LAMB WITH GARLIC

1360g (3 lb) leg of lamb
4 medium potatoes
3 onions
2 cloves garlic
285ml (½ pint) meat stock
5mg (1 tspn) rosemary
5mg (1 tspn) thyme
salt
freshly milled black pepper

Cut the garlic into small slivers and, using a sharp knife, make slits at 2-inch intervals all over the leg and insert the garlic into the slits. Rub the herbs all over the leg and place it in a roasting tin in pre-heated oven, gas mark 8, 450°F (230°C) for 30 minutes. Meanwhile peel and slice the onions

78

and potatoes, placed in a large bowl, and season with salt and pepper. Layer the potatoes and onions around the leg in the tin, pour the hot stock over the vegetables, and return the tin to the oven for a further 1½ hours, reducing the temperature if the potatoes seem to be browning too quickly.

Serve with fresh mint sauce and vegetables or a salad. This is a delicious way of serving a joint without gravy.

Serves 4   Cal: 300   S: 5   C: 90.

(Assumes 115g (4 oz) portions of lean meat)

MINCED MEAT DISHES

When using minced beef in recipes try to buy good quality mince that is not too fatty. Alternatively buy chuck steak or stewing steak, cut off all the visible fat, and mince the meat yourself.

The following recipe is a less fattening variation on classical Spaghetti Bolognese. The calorie savings come from using only 5ml (one teaspoon) instead of 15ml (one tablespoon) of oil and avoiding flour to thicken the sauce.

SPAGHETTI BOLOGNESE

285mg (10 oz) spaghetti
225mg (8 oz) lean minced beef
225mg (8 oz) tinned tomatoes
30ml (2 tbspns) tomato puree
1 small onion
1 clove garlic, crushed
30ml (2 tbspns) red wine
5ml (1 tspn) olive oil
5mg (1 tspn) dried basil
salt
freshly milled black pepper

Bolognese sauce:
Heat the oil in a thick-based saucepan, add the onion (finely

chopped) and garlic, and fry gently for 5 minutes. Turn up the heat and add the meat to brown it, stirring it all the time with a wooden spoon. Pour off any excess fat. Add the tomatoes, tomatoe puree, wine, basil, salt and pepper, give it all a good stir, turn the heat down, put the lid on, and simmer gently for 30 minutes. If you want a thicker sauce take the lid off and allow to bubble gently for a further 20 minutes.

Spaghetti:
Meanwhile, in a large open pan bring some salted water to the boil and add the spaghetti. Boil the spaghetti for 20 minutes until it is tender but not soggy, and then drain it.

Serve the spaghetti with the Bolognese sauce poured over it.

Serves 4   Cal: 430   S: 1   C: 30.

The next three dishes are ideal both for indoor and outdoor cooking on a barbecue.

HOME-MADE BEEFBURGERS

These really are so different from and so much more delicious than the bought variety that it is worth making them at least once just to convince yourself that the effort is worthwhile. And if you have a food processor it takes only seconds to prepare them Adults usually love them, especially if they are grilled over an outdoor barbecue. Although it is a matter of personal taste we find them tastier and more enjoyable than expensive grilled steak. But children used to commercial burgers may not take instantly to them but they soon develop a taste for them.

340mg (12 oz) lean minced beef
1 onion
30g (1 oz) wholemeal breadcrumbs
15ml (1 tbspn) tomato puree
1 egg white
30g (2 tbspns) fresh parsley
or

5mg (1 tspn) dried mixed herbs
2.5ml (½ tspn) Worcestershire sauce
salt
freshly milled black pepper

Chop the onion finely and beat the egg white lightly. Place all the ingredients (except the egg white) in a basin and stir well. Add the egg white to the mixture to bind the ingredients together. Divide into 4 portions and shape into 4 meat rounds and grill for about 5 minutes on each side.

Serve with Barbecue Sauce (recipe on page 126) or grilled tomatoes and a jacket potato.

Serves 4   Cal: 220   S: 1   C: 50.

OTHER MEAT DISHES

The next dish has similar calorie savings to the previous dish, namely 5ml (one *teaspoon*) flour to thicken the sauce. These are good principles which apply to a wide range of dishes, including almost all meat-casserole dishes. In addition low-fat natural yoghurt is used instead of the more traditional larger quantity of soured cream, a good principle to apply to most savoury dishes requiring cream.

LAMB KEBAB

455g (1 lb) leg of lamb
1 onion
1 green pepper
4 small tomatoes
2 cloves garlic, crushed
5g (1 tspn) dried mixed herbs
juice of 2 lemons
salt
freshly milled black pepper

Cut all the visible fat off the lamb and cut the meat into large cubes. Place the meat in a bowl, add the garlic and herbs, and season with salt and pepper. Pour the lemon juice over the mixture. Peel the onion and cut into quarters. Cut the green pepper into even-sized pieces. Add the onion and pepper to the meat mixture and stir well. Cover with cling film and leave for a few hours to marinade.

Take a skewer and thread the meat on to it, alternating with a piece of onion and a piece of pepper, until the skewer is nearly full. Do the same with three more skewers and put a tomato on to the end of each skewer. Grill each skewer under a pre-heated grill, turning frequently, for 15 to 20 minutes, until the meat is well done.

These kebabs are also delicious cooked on a barbecue when they can be served with a jacket potato and barbecue sauce (see recipe on page 126).

Serves 4   Cal: 235   S: 5   C: 90.

BEEF KEBABS

455g (1 lb) rump steak
2 onions
1 green pepper
1 red pepper
115g (4 oz) button mushrooms
225ml (8 oz) tomato juice
2 cloves garlic, crushed
5g (1 tspn) dried mixed herbs
15ml (1 tbspn) soy sauce
salt
freshly milled black pepper

Cut all the visible fat off the steak and cut the meat into large cubes. Mix together the tomato juice, garlic, herbs, soy sauce, salt and pepper. Place the meat in a bowl, pour over the tomato juice mixture, cover with cling film, and marinade for several hours, turning the meat from time to time. Meanwhile peel the onions and cut into quarters. Slice the stalk end off the peppers, remove the cores and seeds, and cut into eight pieces.

When marinaded drain the steak. Take a skewer and thread the meat on to it, alternating with a piece of onion, a piece of pepper and a mushroom, until the skewer is nearly full. Do the same with three more skewers. Grill each skewer under a pre-heated grill, turning frequently, for 15 to 20 minutes, until the meat is well done.

These kebabs are also delicious cooked on a barbecue when they can be served with a jacket potato and barbecue sauce (see recipe on page 126).

Serves 4   Cal: 285   S: 2   C: 65.

GOULASH

570g (1¼ lb) chuck steak, diced
400g (14 oz) tinned tomatoes
70ml (2½ oz) low-fat natural yoghurt
2 onions, sliced
1 pepper (green or red)
1 clove garlic
5ml (1 tspn) olive oil
paprika
salt
freshly milled black pepper

Pour the oil into a heavy-based casserole, turn up the heat and add the meat, garlic and onions and stir until brown. Add the paprika, stir well, and then add the tomatoes. Add the salt and pepper, allow to simmer, cover and then place in the middle of a pre-heated oven, gas mark 2, 300°F (150°C), for 1¾ hours. Meanwhile cut the pepper in half, remove the seeds, cut it into 1½ to 2-inch strips and add it to the goulash at the end of the 1¾ hours. Cook for a further 45 minutes. Just before the end of cooking stir in the yoghurt and sprinkle a little more paprika over the meat.

Serve immediately from the casserole with rice or a salad.

Serves 4   Cal: 290   S: 3   C: 85.

BEEF AND WINE CASSEROLE

455g (1 lb) braising steak
2 onions

2 carrots
2 sticks celery
115g (4 oz) mushrooms
2 cloves garlic, crushed
2.5g (½ tspn) dried thyme
285ml (½ pint) red wine
1 beef stock cube

Cut off all the visible fat from the meat. Cut the meat into chunky cubes and gently fry in a non-stick pan until brown. Meanwhile chop all the vegetables and then add to the browned meat and sauté for about 5 minutes. Add the rest of the ingredients, stir well, and cover with a close-fitting lid. Place in the middle of a pre-heated oven, gas mark 3, 325°F (160°C), for 3½ hours.

Serves 4   Cal: 265   S: 2   C: 65.

CHILI CON CARNE

455g (1 lb) lean minced beef
2 onions
1 green pepper
396g (15½ oz) can red kidney beans
5g (1 tspn) chilli powder
salt

Fry the meat in a non-stick pan until brown. Meanwhile peel and chop the onions, slice the stalk end off the pepper, remove the core and seeds, and chop. Add the onions and pepper to the meat, then cover and cook gently for a few minutes. Add the chilli and fry for one minute, stirring all the while. Add the tomatoes and salt, then cover again and simmer for 25 minutes. Drain the kidney beans and add to the mixture and cook for a further 5 minutes.

Serves 4   Cal: 395   S: 2   C: 65.

STUFFED PEPPERS

4 green peppers
340mg (12 oz) lean minced beef

115g (4 oz) mushrooms
2 carrots
396g (14 oz) tinned tomatoes
2 small onions
2 cloves garlic, crushed
pinch mixed dried herbs
285ml (½ pint) stock
salt
freshly milled black pepper

Fry the beef in its own fat in a non-stick pan. Meanwhile grate the carrots, chop the mushrooms, finely chop the onions, and slice the stalk off the peppers and remove the cores and seeds. Drain off the fat from the beef and add the onions, carrots, mushrooms and garlic. Cook on a low heat until the onions are soft, then add the tomatoes (but not the juice), the herbs and seasoning. Stuff the peppers with the beef and vegetable mixture, then place the peppers in a dish and pour over the juice of the tomatoes and stock. Cover and cook gently in an oven, gas mark 2, 350°F (180°C), for 45 minutes.

Serves 4   Cal: 235   S: 1   C: 50.

On the 3D Diet pork should not be eaten very often. But for the occasional treat the following recipe is simple, yet delicious.

PORK STEAK WITH STUFFING MIX

1 pork chop or pork steak
15g (1 tbspn) sage and onion stuffing mix

Cut all the visible fat off the pork, sprinkle with the stuffing mix, and bake in the oven, gas mark 6, 400°F (200°C), for about 45 minutes.

Serve with apple sauce and a small portion of mashed potatoes and peas.

Serves 1   Cal: 180   S: 3   C: 75.

BAKED GAMMON WITH PINEAPPLE

4 85g (3 oz) lean gammon steaks
4 pineapple rings (canned in their own juice)
140ml (5 oz) low-fat natural yoghurt
7.5g ($\frac{1}{4}$ oz) Flora margarine
2.5g ($\frac{1}{2}$ tspn) made English mustard
40g (3 tbspns) chopped parsley
salt
freshly milled black pepper

Cut off the visible fat from the meat. Grease a shallow oven-proof dish with the margarine, and place the gammon in the dish. Mix together the yoghurt, mustard, parsley, salt and pepper, and pour over the gammon. Cover with foil and bake in the oven, gas mark 3, 160°F (325°C), for 30 minutes.

Serve garnished with a pineapple ring on each steak.

Serves 4   Cal: 195   S: 3   C: 15.

VEAL IN BREADCRUMBS

1 escalope of veal
30g (1 oz) breadcrumbs
1 egg white
30g (1 oz) Flora
$\frac{1}{4}$ lemon (to garnish)

Beat the egg white and then dip the veal in it. Then dip the veal in the breadcrumbs, pressing the breadcrumbs firmly to the meat. Leave to set in a fridge for about an hour. Melt the margarine in a non-stick frying pan and fry the veal for about 5 minutes on each side.

Garnish with lemon and serve with broccoli and carrots.

Serves 1   Cal: 255   S: 4   C: 65.

CHAPTER 14

Fish Main Courses

Fish can play a very important part in any diet as it is a good source of protein. In particular white fish, such as haddock, cod, plaice and sole, is low in saturated fats and cholesterol (although whiting, also a white fish, is the exception in that it is relatively high in cholesterol). Herring, mackerel, salmon and tuna are more oily and so should be eaten less often and more sparingly.

White fish is also low in calories provided that it is not fried or served in rich creamy sauces, but grilled or baked with just a little lemon juice. For example, a 170g (6 oz) portion of plaice fried in batter has 475 calories, whereas the same portion grilled contains less than 160 calories.

COD WITH CUCUMBER

4 170g (6 oz) cod steaks
170g (6 oz) cucumber
1 lemon
55g (2 oz) cottage cheese
140g (5 oz) low-fat natural yoghurt
salt
freshly milled black pepper

Grate the lemon and then squeeze the juice from it. Place the fish in an ovenproof dish and add the lemon rind and juice. Cover and cook in a preheated oven, gas mark 4, 350°F (180°C), for 25 minutes. Drain off any excess liquid. Dice the cucumber and mix it with the cheese, yoghurt, salt

and pepper. Heat the mixture and serve on top of the fish.
Serve garnished with sliced cucumber and parsley.

Serves 4   Cal: 180   S: ½   C: 85.

BAKED COD

4 (170g, 6 oz each) cod
1 green pepper
2 celery sticks
4 tomatoes
1 onion
1 clove garlic, crushed
2.5g (½ tspn) mixed herbs
10g (2 tspns) lemon juice
15g ½ oz) Flora
freshly milled black pepper
parsley

Place the fish in a shallow ovenproof dish and sprinkle with
the lemon juice and pepper. Prepare and chop the vegetables
and fry gently for 10 minutes. Spoon the vegetable mixture
over the fish, cover with foil, and cook in a moderate oven,
gas mark 4, 350°F (180°C), for 30 minutes.

Serve garnished with parsley and with new potatoes or
jacket potato.

Serves 4   Cal: 180   S: 1   C: 85.

SPICEY HADDOCK PARCELS

4 170g (6 oz) haddock fillets
225 (8 oz) mushrooms
2.5g (½ tspn) ground ginger
10g (2 tspns) soy sauce
40ml (4 dessertspns) lemon juice
30g (1 oz) Flora
salt
freshly milled black pepper

88

Remove the skin from the fish. Take 4 pieces of foil large enough to wrap each fillet of haddock in and place a fillet on each. Slice the mushrooms. Mix together the lemon juice, ginger, soy sauce and margarine. Put one-quarter of the mixture on top of each fillet and then place the mushrooms evenly on top. Season with salt and pepper and fold over the foil to make 4 parcels. Bake in the oven, gas mark 4, 350°F (180°C), for 40 minutes.

Serve with brown rice and green salad.

Serves 4   Cal: 230   S: 1   C: 100.

HADDOCK IN PARSLEY SAUCE

4 170g (6 oz) haddock fillets
285ml (10 oz) low-fat natural yoghurt
20ml (4 tspns) lemon juice
60g (4 tbspns) chopped parsley
salt
freshly milled black pepper

Poach the fish in a little water or grill for 10 to 15 minutes until tender. To make the sauce mix the yoghurt and lemon juice together and carefully heat but do not allow to boil. Season the mixture and add the chopped parsley.

Serve the fish with the sauce spooned over it.

Serves 4   Cal: 205   S: ½   C: 100.

GRILLED SOLE WITH GRAPES

4 170g (6 oz) lemon soles
115g (4 oz) green grapes
60ml (4 tbspns) lemon juice
30g (1 oz) Flora
chopped parsley
freshly milled black pepper

Dot each sole with one-quarter of the margarine and season with pepper. Grill for about 10 minutes, turning once.

Meanwhile halve the grapes and remove the pips. When the fish is cooked serve with lemon juice and chopped parsley sprinkled over it and garnish with grapes.

Serve with mixed salad and new potatoes.

Serves 4 Cal: 230 S: ½ C: 100.

OVEN FRIED FISH

4 (4 oz) fillets of cod or haddock
115g (4 oz) wholemeal breadcrumbs
1 egg white, beaten
30g (1 oz) Flora

Dry the fish well and dip into the egg white and then the breadcrumbs. Grease a baking sheet with half the margarine, then arrange the fish on it and dot the top with the remaining margarine. Bake in a hot oven, gas mark 8, 450°F (230°C), for 12 to 15 minutes.

Serve garnished with slices of lemon.

Serves 4 Cal: 215 S: 4 C: 60.

FILLET OF SOLE WITH MUSHROOMS

4 115g (4 oz) fillets of sole
225g (8 oz) mushrooms
1 onion
60ml (4 tbspns) lemon juice
15g (½ oz) Flora
15g (1 tbspn) chopped parsley
salt
freshly milled black pepper

Peel and chop the onion and slice the mushrooms and gently fry in the margarine until lightly browned. Place the fillets in a heavy-based casserole with the onion and mushrooms over and between the fish. Sprinkle with the parsley, salt

and pepper and pour over the lemon juice. Cover and
simmer for 25 minutes.

Serves 4   Cal: 145   S: 1   C: 65.

The next two recipes use fish which are not quite so
desirable with regard to cholesterol, but all are delicious
and, used on occasion, do help to ring the changes.

MACKEREL WITH LEMON

4 medium 115g (4 oz) mackerel
2 onions
60ml (4 tbspns) lemon juice
2 bay leaves
15g (1 tbspn) dried mixed herbs
freshly milled black pepper

Ask your fishmonger to clean and gut the fish for you. Chop
the onions. Place the mackerel in a baking dish and cover
with the onions, lemon juice, bay leaves, herbs and pepper.
Cover tightly with foil and cook in a moderate oven, gas
mark 5, 375°F (190°C), for 40 minutes until the fish is
cooked.

Serve hot, each portion garnished with a slice of lemon.

Serves 4   Cal: 265:   S: 5   C: 90.

For a special summer evening meal or Sunday lunch it is
occasionally worth the extra calories (although do make
adjustments to your calorie intake the rest of the day).

OVEN BAKED SALMON STEAKS

4 115g (4 oz) salmon steaks
60ml (4 tbspns) lemon juice
2 bay leaves, broken into 4
30g (1 oz) Flora

Take 4 pieces of foil and place a salmon steak on each one. Dot with the margarine, sprinkle with juice and put half a bay leaf on each. Wrap the foil over the top of each parcel, place on a baking tray, and cook in a cool oven, gas mark 1, 275°F (140°C) for 25 minutes.

When cool remove the skin and serve with a mixed salad.

Serves 4   Cal: 285   S: 5   C: 90.

CHAPTER 15

Salads

SIDE SALADS

When preparing the ingredients for salads always leave the skins on the fruit and vegetables wherever possible as they provide useful roughage.

CUCUMBER SALAD WITH MINT

1 small cucumber
1 small onion
15g (1 tbspn) fresh chopped mint
140ml (5 oz) low-fat natural yoghurt
salt
freshly milled black pepper

Slice the cucumber and onion and put it into a serving bowl. Add the mint to the yoghurt and season with salt and pepper. Pour the yoghurt mixture over the cucumber, mix well and chill.

Serve as a side salad with a meat dish.-

Serves 4   Cal: 25:   S: ½   C: 2.

MUSHROOM MARINADE

225g (8 oz) button mushrooms
1 clove garlic (crushed)
5g (1 tspn) chopped parsley
15ml (1 tbspn) tomato puree
85ml (3 oz) white wine vinegar
5ml (1 tspn) Worcestershire sauce
2.5g (½ tspn) mustard powder

93

2.5ml (½ tspn) liquid sweetener
55ml (2 oz) water
salt
freshly milled black pepper

Slice the mushrooms and place them in a bowl. Mix all the marinade ingredients together and pour over the mushrooms. Season to taste. Cover with clear food wrap and leave in the fridge to marinade overnight. Give the mushrooms a good stir around two or three times while marinading. Next day drain off the liquid, put the mushrooms into a serving dish and sprinkle with parsley.

This salad can be served either as a starter or as a salad accompaniment.

Serves 4   Cal: 9   S: 0   C: 0.

CARROT SALAD

4 large carrots
55g (2 oz) seedless raisins
30g (1 tbspn) chopped parsley
15ml (½ tbspn) lemon juice
salt
pepper

Peel and grate the carrots. Put the carrots into a bowl, add the raisins and parsley, sprinkle on the lemon juice, and give the ingredients a good stir.

Serve as a side dish with meat or fish.

Serves 4   Cal: 40   S: 0   C: 0.

APPLE AND CABBAGE SLAW

1 small white cabbage
3 red apples
15ml (1 tbspn) lemon juice
40ml (3 tbsns) low calorie mayonnaise (see recipe, page 125)
40ml (3 tbspns) low-fat natural yoghurt

Shred the cabbage finely and put it into a bowl. Core the apples and slice them thinly. Dip them in the lemon juice to prevent browning and add them to the cabbage. Mix the low calorie mayonnaise with the yoghurt and gently stir into the apple and cabbage mixture.

Serves 4   Cal: 65   S: ½   C: 3.

GREEN SALAD

1 lettuce
4 spring onions
15g (1 tbspn) chopped parsley
1 clove garlic (crushed)
1 bunch watercress
30ml (2 tbspns) home-made low-calorie vinaigrette dressing
   (see recipe, page 125)
salt
pepper

Make up the vinaigrette dressing, add the crushed garlic, seasoning and parsley, and allow to stand for about an hour. In a salad bowl mix together the lettuce, spring onion and watercress. Pour over the dressing and turn the salad gently so that it all becomes evenly coated.

Serve with a meat or a fish dish.

Serves 4   Cal: 15   S: ½   C: ½.

RED PEPPER AND BEANSHOOT SALAD

1 red pepper
225g (8 oz) beanshoots
30ml (2 tbspns) home-made low-calorie vinaigrette dressing
   (see recipe, page 125)

Finely slice the pepper and put it into a bowl with the beanshoots. Add the vinaigrette dressing and toss well.

Serve with a meat or a fish dish.

Serves 4   Cal: 20   S: ½   C: ½.

TOMATO SALAD

See chapter 11 page 69

CELERY, RADISH AND GREEN PEPPER SALAD

4 sticks celery
12 radishes
1 green pepper
15ml (1 tbspn) home-made low-calorie vinaigrette dressing
(see recipe, page 125) or lemon juice

Slice the celery into small even pieces, and slice the radishes and green pepper. Mix together in a bowl and add vinaigrette or lemon juice.

Serve as an accompaniment to snacks or main meals.

Serves 4   Cal: 5-10   S: ½   C: ½.

The above salads can be varied to your own personal tastes and they all form very tasty accompaniments to a main meal. The recipes which follow are for more substantial main salad meals or snacks.

A recipe for Potato Salad may seem a little out of place in a book such as this one. But a home-made potato salad is so superior to any of the calorie and cholesterol-laden bought varieties that if it is consumed in moderate amounts you can feel quite justified in eating it occasionally. Do use good quality potatoes and leave the skins *on*.

POTATO SALAD

455g (1 lb) new potatoes
15ml (1 tbspn) low fat natural yoghurt
15ml (1 tbspn) home-made low-calorie mayonnaise (see recipe, page 125)
15ml (1 tbspn) wine vinegar
15g (1 tbspn) chopped parsley *or* chopped mint
salt
freshly milled black pepper

Wash the potatoes and cook gently in boiling, slightly salted, water for 20 minutes. Strain and cut into large cubes, pour the vinegar over the hot potatoes and add pepper. Gently turn the potatoes in the vinegar. When cold add the yoghurt and mayonnaise, sprinkle with parsley or mint, stir carefully to mix well, cover with plastic film and chill.

Serve a heaped tablespoon with any other chosen salad.

For each heaped tablespoon: Cal: 65-95   S: ½   C: ½.

Other fillers that may be used instead of potato salad are those wonderfully filling and nutritious pulses. Red kidney beans, green beans, butter beans, canellini beans – a sprinkling of these add interest, texture and protein to any salad at a cost of, in the case of 30g (1 oz) red kidney beans, 30 calories.

RED KIDNEY BEAN SALAD

170g (6 oz) red kidney beans (cooked or canned)
6 sticks celery
¼ onion
½ green pepper
15ml (1 tbspn) home-made low-calorie vinaigrette dressing
    (see recipe, page 125)

Chop the celery and green pepper. Slice the onion into rings. Rinse the kidney beans. Mix all the ingredients together with the vinaigrette.

Serves 4   Cal: 50   S: ½   C: ½.

RED CABBAGE CRUNCHY SALAD

85g (3 oz) red cabbage
3 sticks celery
1 apple
½ green pepper
30ml (1 oz) low-fat natural yoghurt
15ml (1 tbspn) home-made low-calorie mayonnaise (see
    recipe, page 125)

Shred the cabbage, chop the celery and green pepper, core and slice the apple (and dip in lemon juice to prevent discoloration) and place the ingredients in a bowl. Add the yoghurt and vinaigrette and toss well.

Serves 4   Cal: 30   S: ½   C: ½.

SALADS AS MAIN COURSES OR SNACKS

PASTA AND CHICKEN SALAD

115g (4 oz) wholewheat pasta rings or shells
225g (8 oz) cooked chicken
2 red apples
2 sticks celery
30ml (2 tbspns) low-cholesterol mayonnaise (see page 125)
15ml (1 tbspn) low-fat natural yoghurt
salt
freshly milled black pepper

Cook the pasta according to the instructions on the packet. Cool it. Remove the skin from the chicken and cut the flesh into bite-size pieces. Core and dice the apple. Chop the celery and mix with the pasta, chicken and apple. Season. Add the mayonnaise mixed with yoghurt and evenly coat the chicken-pasta mixture.

Serve on a bed of lettuce.

Serves 4   Cal: 235   S: 1   C: 40.

CURRIED CHICKEN SALAD

340g (12 oz) cooked chicken
30ml (2 tbspns) low-fat natural yoghurt
salt
5g (1 tspn) curry paste
15g (1 tbspn) mango chutney
1 lettuce
12 slices cucumber
2 tomatoes, sliced

98

Skin the chicken and cut into bite-size pieces. Mix the yoghurt, curry paste and chutney together. Arrange the lettuce leaves, cucumber and tomatoes on to four plates. Divide the chicken pieces equally and arrange on top of the lettuce. Coat the chicken with the curry mixture.

Serves 4   Cal: 135   S: 1   C: 65.

BEEF SALAD

85g (3 oz) lean roast beef
1 tomato
1 lettuce
5ml (1 tspn) home-made low-calorie vinaigrette dressing
   (see recipe, page 125)
radishes
spring onions
celery

Remove all the visible fat from the beef. Arrange the meat on a plate and serve with a salad made with a tomato and any amount of the other salad vegetables as you like. Sprinkle the salad with low-calorie vinaigrette.

Serves 1   Cal: 180   S: 2   C: 50.

TUNA SALAD

1 198g (7 oz) tin tuna *in brine*
1 lettuce
2 tomatoes
½ cucumber
4 spring onions

Arrange a couple of lettuce leaves on each plate. Slice the tomatoes and cucumber and arrange these on top of the lettuce. Flake the tuna fish and divide it between each plate. Chop the onions and sprinkle over the top.

Serves 4   Cal: 30   S: 2   C: 30.

TUNA AND PASTA SALAD

½ tin, ie 99g (3½ oz) tuna *in brine*
115g (4 oz) wholewheat pasta rings or shells
30ml (2 tbspns) home-made low-calorie vinaigrette dressing
(see page 125)

Cook the wholewheat pasta according to the instructions on
the packet. Drain and toss in the vinaigrette dressing. Drain
the tuna and flake. Add the tuna to the pasta and chill.

Serve on a bed of lettuce with a few radishes as a garnish.

Serves 4   Cal: 135   S: 1   C: 15.

CHILLI BEAN AND FRANKFURTER SALAD

1 420g (15 oz) can red kidney beans, drained
1 red pepper
1 green pepper
1 onion
2 tomatoes
1 head chicory or lettuce
4 Frankfurters

Dressing:
30ml (2 tbspns) home-made low-calorie vinaigrette dressing
(see page 125)
2.5ml (½ tspn) Tabasco sauce
pinch chilli powder
salt
freshly milled black pepper

Peel and slice the onion, and slice the peppers and tomatoes.
Drain and rinse the kidney beans. Cut the Frankfurters into
bite-size pieces. Put all the ingredients into a large bowl.
Mix together the ingredients of the dressing and pour over
the bean mixture. Stir well and chill.

Serve on a bed of lettuce or chicory.

Serves 4   Cal: 175   S: 2   C: 8.

APRICOT SALAD

8 fresh apricots
½ lettuce
225g cottage cheese

Chop the apricots and mix into the cottage cheese. Arrange two or three lettuce leaves on four plates and divide the cheese mixture into four. Put a portion on to the lettuce on each plate.

Serve with a wholemeal bread roll or a small portion of potato salad.

When apricots are not available substitute tinned pineapple canned in its own juice (*not* syrup) or chopped apple or even a little chopped melon. The addition of fruit turns cottage cheese into a much more enjoyable experience.

Serves 4   Cal: 65   S: 1   C: 5.

CUCUMBER JELLY

1 cucumber
2 lemons
5g (1 tspn) chopped mint
5g (1 tspn) chopped thyme
285g (10 oz) low-fat natural yoghurt
15g (½ oz) powdered gelatine
salt
freshly milled black pepper

Cut 2.5cm (one inch) off the end of the cucumber, and thinly slice and arrange the slices in the bottom of a glass bowl. Peel the rest of the cucumber and dice. Grate the rind from the lemons and extract the juice. Dissolve the gelatine in 140ml (¼ pint) cold water in a basin standing over a pan of simmering water. Stir in the lemon juice and rind, pour a thin layer of the lemon jelly into the glass bowl, and allow to set. Keeping the rest of the lemon mixture over the hot water stir it from time to time so that it does not set. When the bottom layer of the jelly is set whisk the yoghurt into the

101

mixture in the basin, stir in the cucumber, mint and thyme, and season. Pour the mixture into the glass bowl and allow to set.

To serve dip the bowl in hot water and turn the jelly on to a plate. If you like, serve with lettuce.

Serves 6   Cal: 35   S: ½   C: 3.

CHAPTER 16

Puddings

Ideally it is best not to have a sweet tooth so that you can avoid puddings which tend to be pretty calorific. However for those who find a sweet ending to a meal a 'must' here are a few suggestions.

BAKED APPLES

4 medium cooking apples
8 black grapes
140ml (¼ pint) dry cider
55ml (4 tbspns) low-fat natural yoghurt
liquid sweetener

Core each apple and make a cut in the skin around the middle. Place the apples in an oven-proof dish. Slice the grapes in half and remove the pips. Push four grape halves into the centre of each apple. Add the liquid sweetener (about 8 drops – more if you have a very sweet tooth) to the cider and pour the cider mixture over the apples. Bake in the oven, gas mark 5, 375°F (190°C), for 45 to 60 minutes until soft.

Serve hot with low-fat natural yoghurt.

Serves 4   Cal: 80   S: ½   C: 1.

SYLLABUB

570ml (1 pint) low-fat natural yoghurt
1 lemon
30ml (2 tbspns) dry sherry
liquid sweetener

Grate the rind of the lemon and squeeeze out the juice. Whisk the yoghurt until it thickens slightly. Slowly mix in the lemon juice and grated rind. Add the sherry and sweeten to taste.

Serve in glass dishes and decorate with a twist of lemon.

Serves 4   Cal: 80   S: ½   C: 9.

PEACH MELBA

55g (2 oz) raspberries
1 peach
2.5ml (½ tspn) liquid sweetener
2.5ml (½ tspn) vanilla essence
1 egg white

Blend together the yoghurt and sweetener and partly, but not completely, freeze in the freezer. Whisk the egg white. Turn the yoghurt mixture into a bowl, add the vanilla essence and egg white, and freeze until firm. Sieve the raspberries to make a smooth puree and blend together with the sweetener to taste. Scoop out the ice-cream and pour over the puree.

Serve decorated with slices of peach.

Serves 2   Cal: 100   S: ½   C: 9.

ORANGE AND RHUBARB

455g (1 lb) rhubarb
2 oranges
liquid or granulated sweetener

Cut the rhubarb into even-sized pieces about one inch long. Peel and slice the oranges. Layer the rhubarb and sliced oranges in casserole dish. Cover and bake in the oven, gas mark 3, 325°F (165°C), until the rhubarb is tender (about 30 minutes). Add the sweetener if required when cooked.

Serve hot or cold.

Serves 4   Cal: 20   S: 0   C: 0.

APPLE MOUSSE

455g (1 lb) cooking apples
30g (2 tbspns) redcurrant jelly
1 egg white
ground cinnamon
100ml (½ teacup) water.

Peel, slice and core the apples, and cook them until tender.
Whilst the fruit is hot add the redcurrant jelly. Liquidise the
apple mixture. Allow the mixture to cool. Whisk the egg
white until it is stiff, and then fold into the apple mixture.
Spoon the mixture into four glass bowls.

Serve chilled with a little cinnamon sprinkled on top.

Serves 4   Cal: 70   S: ½   C: ½.

CHOCOLATE SOUFFLE

30g (2 tbspns) cocoa powder
30g (2 tbspns) cornflour
10ml (2 tspns) liquid sweetner
430ml (¾ pint) skimmed milk
55ml (4 extra tbspns) skimmed milk
3 egg whites
5ml (1 tspn) vanilla essence

Heat the 430ml (¾ pint) of skimmed milk. Carefully mix the
cornflour, cocoa powder and sweetener with the 55ml (4
tablespoons) of cold skimmed milk to form a smooth paste.
Gently add to the hot milk and cook, stirring all the time,
until the mixture thickens. Remove from the heat and allow
to cool. Whip the egg whites with the vanilla essence until
stiff and fold into the cold chocolate mixture. Spoon the
mixture into a serving dish.

Serve chilled and decorated with a little grated chocolate.

Serves 4   Cal: 90   S: ½   C: 2.

STRAWBERRY CHEESECAKE

Base:
6 low calorie digestive biscuits
55g (2 oz) Flora

Filling:
1 packet strawberry jelly
225g (8 oz) cottage cheese
55g (2 oz) granulated sweetener
fresh strawberries (if in season) or satsumas to decorate

Melt the margarine. Crush the biscuits, stir into the margarine, and press into the bottom of a 7-inch flan ring on a serving plate. Chill until firm. Using a measuring jug dissolve the jelly so that it makes 140ml ($\frac{1}{4}$ pint) of liquid. Allow to cool. Sieve the cheese and mix in the granulated sweetener. Stir in the jelly mixture. Pour over the base and chill until set. Remove the flan ring.

Serve decorated with strawberries or satsumas.

Serves 6   Cal: 155   S: 2   C: 5.

FRUIT JELLY

1 pineapple jelly
140g (5 oz) low-fat natural yoghurt
4 orange twists
190ml ($\frac{1}{3}$ pint) orange juice
140ml ($\frac{1}{4}$ pint) water

Dissolve the jelly in the water. Add the orange juice. Place in a bowl and chill until it is just beginning to set. Whisk in the yoghurt until blended. Pour into four glass bowls and allow to set.

Serve chilled and decorate with orange twists.

Serves 4   Cal: 60   S: $\frac{1}{2}$ C: 2.

FRUIT PAVLOVA or SLIMMERS' MERINGUE

1 410g (14$\frac{1}{2}$ øz) tin of fruit salad in unsweetened syrup *or*
  home-made fruit salad (see next recipe)

3 large egg whites
5ml (1 tspn) cream of tartar
45g (3 tbspns) skimmed milk powder
30g (6 tspns) granulated sweetener
6 sprigs mint

Whisk the egg whites, add the cream of tartar, and continue whisking until the mixture stiffens and peaks form. Add the skimmed milk powder and sweetener until peaks form again. Draw a circle round an 8-inch plate on a sheet of non-stick paper. Place on a baking sheet and spread (or pipe) the mixture smoothly in the circle. Cook in a pre-heated oven, gas mark 1, for one hour. Cool, then loosen carefully with a palette knife and lift and place on a serving dish. Drain the fruit salad and pile on top of the meringue, and top with the sprigs of mint.

Serves 4   Cal: 115   S: ½   C: 2.

FRUIT SALAD

2 oranges
2 apples
1 banana
1 pear
¼ melon
115g (4 oz) strawberries
55g (2 oz) grapes (preferably seedless)
55ml (2 oz) fresh orange juice
liquid or granulated sweetener to taste

Peel, slice and chop the fruit, as appropriate, and mix together. Add the orange juice to stop the fruit from discolouring and also to provide necessary fluid. Taste and sweeten as you wish.

Serves 4   Cal: 75   S: 0   C: 0.

The following dish is one of our favourites and is always a great hit at dinner parties.

CREPES SUZETTE

115g (4 oz) plain flour or part plain and part wholemeal
1 egg white
285ml (½ pint) skimmed milk (or 2 tbspns skimmed milk
    powder dissolved in 285ml, ½ pint, water)
juice and finely grated rind of 2 medium oranges
30ml (2 tbspns) Cointreau or Grand Marnier
15ml (1 tbspn) cooking brandy
3 tbspns granulated sweetener

Make the batter *either* by sieving the flour and half the
sweetener into a mixing bowl and adding the milk and egg
and mixing it to a smooth batter *or* by mixing the same
ingredients in a blender or food mixer. Using a non-stick
frying pan cook wafer-thin pancakes, using a *minute* amount
of polyunsaturated oil to grease the pan. If you use a 7-inch
pan you should get about 9 pancakes. Stack them using
grease-proof paper to prevent them sticking to each other.

Next, make the Suzette sauce by mixing together the rest
of the sweetener, orange juice and rind, and orange liqueur.
Place the sauce in a fridge until needed when it is then
placed in a large frying pan and gently heated. Put a
pancake in the pan, let it warm through, and then form a
triangle of it by folding it in half and then half again. Slide it
out to the edge of the pan, add the next pancake, and repeat
the process. Do the same for all the pancakes. Place the
pancakes side by side in a flameproof dish and place in a
pre heated oven, gas mark 7, 425°F (220°C), for 10 minutes.

To serve, bring to the table, pour the brandy from a
well-heated ladle over the pancakes, and ignite (having first
switched off the room lights!). Spoon the liqueur and sauce
over the pancakes, and serve.

*Serves 4 to 6 depending on greed!   Cal: 70   S: ½   C: ½ each
pancake.*

ORANGE SORBET

1 170g (6 oz) can unsweetened orange juice
2 tbspns lemon juice

1 egg white
5ml (1 tspn) liquid sweetener
285ml (½ pint) water

Mix together the orange juice, lemon juice, sweetener and water and pour into a suitable container to place in a freezer (such as an ice-cube tray or an old ice-cream tub) and freeze until just firm. Remove from the freezer and tip the mixture into a bowl and mash with a fork or potato masher until the crystals are broken down. Whisk the egg white until stiff and fold into the orange mixture. Once again pour the mixture into a container and freeze until firm.

Before serving place the mixture in a fridge for about 20 minutes to allow it to soften slightly. Serve in glass dishes and decorate with a twist of orange or sprig of mint.

Serves 4   Cal: 15   S: 0   C: 0.

FRUIT COMPOTES

Compotes are a very easy and pleasant way to end a meal. Any combination of fruit to your own taste can be cooked gently in a little water and, if wished, added sweetener. Here are a few of our suggestions but there is no reason why you cannot mix any fruits that are in season and readily available.

Compotes can be served either on their own or, if your calorie allowance allows, with low-fat natural yoghurt or custard made with skimmed milk and artificial sweetener.

APPLE AND BLACKBERRY COMPOTE

225g (8 oz) apples
225g (8 oz) blackberries
140ml (¼ pint) water
liquid sweetener to taste

Peel and slice the apples and wash the blackberries. Put the fruit in a pan with the water, cook gently until the fruit is soft, and add the sweetener.

Serve hot or cold.

Serves 4   Cal: 40   S: 0   C: 0.

APPLE AND LEMON COMPOTE

455g (1 lb) cooking apples
30ml (2 tbspns) lemon juice
2 cloves
285ml ¼ to ½ pint) water
liquid sweetener to taste

Peel, slice and core the apples and place in a pan with the lemon juice, water and cloves. Cook gently until the fruit is soft, and then remove the cloves.

Serve hot or cold.

Serves 4   Cal: 50   S: 0   C: 0.

PLUM AND PEAR COMPOTE

225g (8 oz) plums
225g (8 oz) pears (peeled and sliced)
140ml (¼ pint) water
cinnamon
liquid sweetener to taste

Halve the plums and remove the stones. Place the plums, pears and water in a pan. Cook gently until the fruit is soft and add the sweetener to taste.

Serve hot or cold with a sprinkling of cinnamon.

Serves 4   Cal: 45   S: 0   C: 0.

HOT FRUIT COMPOTE

2 large oranges
2 large pears
1 apple
225g (8 oz) fresh or frozen raspberries

140ml (¼ pint) water
liquid sweetener to taste
cinnamon

Peel the oranges and divide into segments. Peel the pears
and apple and cut into slices. Place the fruit in a saucepan
with the water and cook gently for about 10 minutes, then
add the sweetener and a sprinkling of cinnamon.

Serve hot with low-fat natural yoghurt or custard made
with skimmed milk and artificial sweetener.

Serves 4   Cal: 55   S: 0   C: 0.

WATERMELON SALAD

½ medium watermelon

Cut the watermelon into chunks. Discard the pips and skin.
Place the chunks in four glass serving dishes.

Serves 4   Cal: 35   S: 0   C: 0.

LEMON JELLY WITH BANANA

1 banana
·1 packet of lemon jelly
juice of 1 lemon

Make the jelly as instructed on the packet. Stir in the lemon
juice and allow to cool. Slice the banana thinly. Pour a layer
of jelly, half an inch to an inch deep, into a mould and allow
to set. Arrange the banana slices over this and then carefully
pour the remaining jelly mixture over the banana. Allow to
set. Unmould to serve.

Serves 4   Cal: 30   S: 0   C: 0.

RASPBERRY SORBET

455g (1 lb) raspberries
2 egg whites
granulated or liquid sweetener

Make a puree out of the raspberries, saving about ten, and then sieve to remove the seeds. Sweeten to taste. Beat the egg whites until stiff and then fold in the puree mixture. Pour into a freezing tray and freeze for about two hours. Turn the mixture into a bowl and mash until smooth. Return it to the freezer and freeze until solid.

Serve decorated with two or three raspberries on each portion.

Serves 4   Cal: 30   S: 0   C: 0.

SUMMER PUDDING

455g (1 lb) mixed summer fruit (such as raspberries, redcurrants, blackcurrants)
115g (4 oz) white bread (thinly sliced, slightly stale
7.5g (¼ oz) St Ivel Gold margarine
30ml (2 tbspns) water
granulated or liquid sweetener

Place the fruit in a saucepan, add the water, cover the pan, and cook gently for 5 minutes. Sweeten to taste and allow to cool. Grease a pudding basin with the margarine. Remove the crusts from the bread and line the basin with some of the slices. Place the fruit in the basin and cover with the rest of the bread. Put a saucer on top of the pudding, put a weight on the saucer, and place in a fridge for at least eight hours before eating.

To serve turn out on to a plate.

Serves 4   Cal: 100   S: ½   C: ½.

WHOLEMEAL YORKSHIRE PUDDING

115g (4 oz) wholemeal flour
1 egg
285ml (½ pint) skimmed milk (or 2 tbspns skimmed milk powder dissolved in 285ml, ½ pint, water)
15g (½ oz) white Flora
salt (just a pinch)

112

Make the batter *either* by sieving the flour into a mixing bowl and adding the milk and egg and mixing to a smooth batter *or* by mixing the same ingredients in a blender or food mixer. Melt the White Flora in a Yorkshire pudding tin in a pre-heated oven, gas mark 7, 425 F (220 C), until the fat is hot. Pour in the batter and cook for about 30 minutes.

Serves 6   Cal: 110   S: ½   C: 14.

CHAPTER 17

All About Spreads

Many people are very confused about the differences between butter and the variety of margarines which are available today.

Butter is made entirely from milk and therefore contains a good deal of both saturated fats and cholesterol. It is also very calorific.

Ordinary margarines, whether hard or soft, are made from a mixture of animal and vegetable oils and contain a little less saturated fats and cholesterol, but they are just as calorific.

Polyunsaturated margarines, such as Flora, have all the animal fats replaced by vegetable oils so that they contain even fewer saturated fats and virtually no cholesterol. But the total fat content is the same and so too are the calories.

Low-fat spreads, such as St Ivel Gold and Outline, contain much less fat, so that both the saturated fat content and calories are greatly reduced. Therefore the slimmer on the 3D Diet should use low-fat spreads wherever possible, eg spread on bread or toast or used in jacket potato. (Our own preference, based on taste, is for St Ivel Gold and this is the one mentioned in various recipes in this book.)

Unfortunately low-fat spreads are not suitable for cooking, especially at high temperatures. The reason for this in the case of St Ivel Gold is that protein has been added and this separates out from the fat. Outline contains water which has a habit of fighting against the oil. Therefore for frying Flora should be used, and a special formulation called White Flora is available.

Content per 100g (3½ oz) butter or margarine

	Total fat g	Sat. fat g	Pro- tein g	Calo- ries
Butter	82	51.8	0.4	740
Average margarine	81	31.2	0.1	730
Flora	81	20.0	0.1	730
St Ivel Gold	41	11.5	7.0	380

CHAPTER 18

Sandwiches and Snacks

First, a brief word on what we mean by 'snacks'. These are *not* things to eat between meals but are the meals themselves. A snack simply denotes a meal which, though nutritious and satisfying, is fairly modest in size. Moreover it can be prepared quickly and easily. And yet, although it can be almost literally 'thrown together' it offers great scope for cullinary imagination.

SANDWICHES

Sandwiches can be varied and nutritious providing the fillings are sensibly thought out. Try to use wholemeal bread and low-fat margarines, such as St Ivel Gold.

The basic method for making each sandwich described is as follows:

Ingredients:
2 slices wholemeal bread
15g (½ oz) St Ivel Gold
filling

Method:
Spread the bread with the margarine. Place the filling on one slice of bread and then put the remaining slice on top. Cut into four and serve.

Everyone has their own favourites, but here are a few suggestions.

CHICKEN AND SALAD SANDWICH

2 slices cooked chicken
1 lettuce leaf
4 slices cucumber

First place the lettuce leaves on one slice of bread, place the chicken on top, and then the cucumber.

Serves 1   Cal: 265   S: 3   C: 35.

CHICKEN AND APPLE AND CABBAGE SLAW SANDWICH

2 slices cooked chicken
30g (1 oz) apple and cabbage slaw (see recipe, page 94)

Serves 1   Cal: 280   S: 3   C: 35.

SALAD SANDWICH

1 tomato, sliced
4 radishes
4 slices cucumber
1 leaf lettuce
sprinkling of cress

Serves 1   Cal: 190   S: 2   C: ½.

CHEESE AND TOMATO SANDWICH

30g (1 oz) Edam cheese, thinly sliced
1 tomato, sliced

Serves 1   Cal: 270   S: 4   C: 20.

TUNA AND CUCUMBER SANDWICH

½ small tin tuna in brine
4 slices cucumber

Serves 1   Cal: 250   S: 4   C: 25.

SARDINE SANDWICH

55g (2 oz) sardines
5ml (1 tspn) lemon juice

Mash the sardine and add the lemon juice.

Serves 1   Cal: 280   S: 5   C: 55.

BEEF AND MUSTARD SANDWICH

55g (2 oz) roast beef, thinly sliced

Make sure that you remove all the visible fat from the meat.

Serves 1   Cal: 290   S: 2   C: 30.

BEEF AND HORSERADISH SANDWICH

55g (2 oz) roast beef, thinly sliced
5mg (1 tspn) horseradish sauce

Make sure that you remove all the visible fat from the meat.

Serves 1   Cal: 290   S: 2   C: 30.

HAM AND GHERKIN SANDWICH

55g (2 oz) lean ham, thinly sliced
2 small gherkins

Make sure that you remove all the visible fat from the meat.

Serves 1   Cal: 250   S: 2   C: 15.

COTTAGE CHEESE, RADISH AND CUCUMBER SANDWICH

55g (2 oz) cottage cheese
4 radishes
4 slices cucumber

Serves 1   Cal: 240   S: 4   C: 6.

COTTAGE CHEESE AND MARMITE SANDWICH

55g (2 oz) cottage cheese
marmite

Serves 1   Cal: 240   S: 4   C: 6.

COTTAGE CHEESE AND PINEAPPLE SANDWICH

55g (2 oz) cottage cheese
1 ring pineapple, fresh or tinned in its own juice (*not* syrup)

Chop up the pineapple and mix it into the cheese.

Serves 1   Cal: 245   S: 4   C: 6.

BANANA SANDWICH

1 banana, sliced

Serves1   Cal: 225   S: 2   C: ½.

PEANUT BUTTER SANDWICH

15g (½ oz) peanut butter

Serves 1   Cal: 275   S: 2   C: ½.

NIBBLES AND DIPS

Raw vegetables and fruit, cut up and attractively arranged,
make marvellous nibbles to dip into when you really don't
feel like having a big sandwich. They are also suitable to add
to a lunchbox to go with a sandwich. A few sliced up salad
ingredients, wrapped in cling film, make a sandwich-based
lunchbox more interesting both for children and adults.

One tip to make the preparation of these snacks quicker
and easier is always to clean and prepare your ingredients as
soon as possible after you have bought them. After washing
radishes, lettuce, celery, and so on, wrap them in cling film
and store in the fridge until you need them when they will
take only seconds to slice and use.

Celery can be used as the basis of many nibbles.

CELERY, COTTAGE CHEESE AND MARMITE NIBBLE

1 stick celery
55g (2 oz) cottage cheese
Marmite

Spread the inside of the celery with marmite and then a layer of cheese. Cut the stick into one inch lengths and you have a very tasty snack.

Serves 1   Cal: 240   S: 1   C: 6.

CELERY, COTTAGE CHEESE AND GHERKIN

1 stick celery
55g (2 oz) cottage cheese
2 small gherkins

Chop the gherkins into small pieces and mix into the cheese. Spread the inside of the celery with cheese and gherkin mix. Cut the stick into one inch lengths.

Serves 1   Cal: 240   S: 1   C: 6.

Experiment with your favourite tastes and find a formula that suits you. Celery spread with a mixture of cottage cheese and pineapple, for example, may be more to your taste.

If your children object to cottage cheese you can use a cheese spread such as Primula or Dairylea. You can use a wide variety of garnishes such as the ones already used with cottage cheese (Marmite, gherkins). Two more examples are described below.

CELERY, CHEESE SPREAD AND RADISHES

1 stick celery
15g (½ oz) cheese spread
4 radishes

Chop the radishes into small pieces and mix into the cheese. Spread the inside of the celery with cheese and radish mix. Cut the stick into one inch lengths.

Serves 1   Cal: 230   S: 2   C: 9.

CELERY, CHEESE SPREAD AND STUFFED OLIVES

1 stick celery

15g (½ oz) cheese spread
3 stuffed olives

Chop the olives into small pieces and mix into the cheese. Spread the inside of the celery with cheese and olive mix. Cut the stick into one inch lengths.

Serves 1   Cal: 230   S: 2   C: 9.

HOT SNACKS

Jacket Potatoes

Hot snacks based on jacket potatoes really are quick, easy and very delicious as well as being good for you. Don't listen to the old-fashioned nonsense about the need to cut out potatoes from your diet if you want to lose weight. A medium-sized potato baked in the oven until it is soft to the touch and then served in any of the following ways is very nutritious without being particularly calorific. But don't forget to eat the skin – it is a very useful source of fibre.

JACKET POTATO AND BAKED BEANS

1 medium potato
1 140g (5 oz) tin baked beans
15g (½ oz) St Ivel Gold
salt
freshly milled black pepper

Cook the potato in the oven, gas mark 6, 400°F (200°C), for 45 to 60 minutes until soft to the touch. Slice the potato in half and mash in a little margarine with the potato, season, and serve with heated baked beans.

Serves 1   Cal: 215   S: 1   C: ½.

JACKET POTATO AND BACON

1 medium potato
2 rashers lean back bacon
15g (½ oz) St Ivel Gold

Cook the potato in the oven, gas mark 6, 400°F (200°C), for 45 to 60 minutes until soft to the touch, and serve with *crispy grilled* bacon.

Serves 1   Cal: 300   S: 2   C: 13.

JACKET POTATO WITH EDAM CHEESE AND APPLE AND CABBAGE SLAW

1 medium potato
30g (1 oz) Edam cheese
30g (1 oz) apple and cabbage slaw
15g (½ oz) St Ivel Gold

Cook the potato in the oven, gas mark 6, 400°F (200°C), for 45 to 60 minutes until soft to the touch, and serve with grated cheese sprinkled on top with apple and cabbage slaw. If you use home-made apple and cabbage slaw dress with a low-calorie dressing. If you use a commercial coleslaw choose one with vinaigrette or a low-calorie dressing (see page 125 in section on Sauces.)

Serves 1   Cal: 115   S: 5   C: 20.

JACKET POTATO WITH COTTAGE CHEESE AND CHIVES

1 medium potato
55g (2 oz) cottage cheese
sprinkling of chives
salt
freshly milled black pepper

Cook the potato in the oven, gas mark 6, 400°F (200°C), for 45 to 60 minutes until soft to the touch. Then scoop out the flesh, mash it together with the cheese and chives, and season. Put the mixture back into the skin and reheat for five minutes before serving with a green salad.

Serves 1   Cal: 143   S: 1   C: 6

JACKET POTATO AND MINCE

1 medium potato
30g (2 tbspns) mince
15g (½ oz) St Ivel Gold

Cook the potato in the oven, gas mark 6, 400°F (200°C), for 45 to 60 minutes until soft to the touch, and serve with mince (see recipe for minced beef under Spaghetti Bolognese on page 79). You may have enough left over from last night's supper to have for a lunchtime snack with a jacket potato.

Serves 1   Cal: 200   S: 2   C: 16.

Pizzas

Pizzas make marvellously quick and easy snacks. There are so many different varieties on the market that we really do not think that it is worth the effort to make your own unless you are blessed with time and a love of cooking. When buying a pizza choose one that is not too laden down with ham or sausages or similar ingredients. Pizzas are ideal served with salads. Calorific content tends to vary on pizzas, but on the whole they are high. Try to eat only a small portion.

Snacks on Toast

CHEESE ON TOAST

115g (4 oz) cottage cheese
2 slices wholemeal bread
15g (½ oz) flour
15g (½ oz) Flora
45ml (3 tbspns) skimmed milk
5mg (1 tspn) mustard
Worcestershire sauce
salt
freshly milled black pepper

Melt the Flora in a saucepan, add the flour and stir in the milk. Cook gently for two minutes, then beat in the cheese and season to taste. To serve pour over the toasted bread.

Serves 2   Cal: 200   S: 2   C: 7.

MUSHROOMS AND TOMATO ON TOAST

4 medium-sized mushrooms
1 tomato
4 slices wholemeal bread
15g (½ oz) Flora
salt
freshly milled black pepper

Slice the mushrooms and tomato and fry them gently in the Flora for about 5 minutes. Season and serve on toasted bread.

Serves 4   Cal: 90   S: 2   C: ½.

CHAPTER 19

Sauces

HOME-MADE LOW-CALORIE VINAIGRETTE DRESSING

40ml (3 tbspns) wine vinegar
15ml (1 tbspn) polyunsaturated oil
5ml (1 tspn) Worcestershire sauce
5g (1 tspn) dry mustard
2 drops liquid sweetener

Put the ingredients into a screw-top jar and shake well.

Cal: 60   S: 1   C: ½ per 30ml (1 oz).

There are two recipes for home-made low-calorie low-cholesterol mayonnaise. The first takes longer to make but is lower in calories than the second. Which you use depends on individual taste and how lazy you are feeling.

HOME-MADE LOW-CALORIE LOW-CHOLESTEROL MAYONNAISE (1)

285ml (½ pint) skimmed milk
15g (½ oz) cornflour
100ml (6 tbspns) polyunsaturated oil
100ml (6 tbspns) vinegar *or* lemon juice
7.5g (1½ tspn) dry mustard
5g (1 tspn) paprika
12 drops liquid sweetener
2.5g (½ tspn) salt

Mix the milk and cornflour together to make a paste in a saucepan and cook until thickened. Place the paste in a bowl, add the mustard, paprika, sweetener and salt, and beat the ingredients until smooth. Gradually add the oil and vinegar (or lemon juice), beating all the time, until the mixture is blended.

Cal: 60   S: ½   C: ½ each 30ml (1 oz).

HOME-MADE LOW-CALORIE LOW-CHOLESTEROL MAYONNAISE (2)

285ml (½ pint) skimmed milk
225ml (8 oz) polyunsaturated oil
40ml (3 tbspns) vinegar *or* lemon juice
7.5g (1½ tspn) dry mustard
5g (1 tspn) paprika
12 drops liquid sweetener
2.5g (½ tspn) salt

Blend all the ingredients together in a food processor or blender into a smooth, thick mixture.

Cal: 105   S: ½   C: ½ each 30ml (1 oz).

Each of these mayonnaises has only a fraction of the saturated fats and cholesterol of an ordinary bought mayonnaise and only about a quarter of the calories. If you feel that making your own mayonnaise is too much bother you can use Flora Sunflower (mayonnaise style) dressing which, though not quite so low in calories, has a highly acceptable taste. Each 30ml (1 oz) has about 150 calories and just over 2g saturated fat.

BARBECUE SAUCE

340g (12 oz) tomato ketchup
2 onions
2 sticks celery
55ml (4 tbspns) vinegar
55ml (4 tbspns) granulated sweetener
10g (2 tspns) dry mustard
55g (2 oz) Flora

juice of 1 lemon
freshly milled black pepper

Chop the onions and celery. Melt the margarine in a large saucepan and fry the onions until they are soft and golden. Add the rest of the ingredients and stir well. Cover and leave on a gentle heat, stirring occasionally, for about 15 minutes. Allow to cool.

This makes about 570g (20 oz) of delicious sauce which will probably be sufficient for several barbecues. It will keep in a fridge for several days.

Cal: 25   S: 5   C: ½ each 30mg (1 oz).

CHAPTER 20

The Drinking Person's Guide to Slimming

On most diets alcohol is banned. There is in fact no logical
reason for this save the fact that alcohol is calorific without
any nutritional benefit. It contains about seven calories
each gram, compared with four calories a gram of carbohydrate or protein, and *nine* calories a gram of fat. Providing
you count it in your total daily calorie allowance there is no
reason why you should deprive yourself of moderate
amounts. In fact some of the recipes in this book contain
alcohol!

If you do have a drink try to avoid adding unnecessary
calories. For example, if you have a gin and tonic use
low-calorie or 'slimline' tonic. If you are faced with a long
evening of drinking remember that a slimline tonic water
without gin looks just like a gin and tonic. And if you 'dress' it
up with Angostura bitters, a slice of lemon and ice it can be
very satisfying.

Avoid, too, those bowls of crisps and peanuts. They are
very fattening and do little to satisfy your hunger.

Calorific value of common alcoholic drinks

DRINK	CALS
Beers (each half-pint):	
brown ale	80
canned bitter	91
draught bitter	91

128

DRINK	CALS
draught mild	71
keg bitter	88
lager	82
pale ale	91
stout	105
stout extra	111
strong ale	204

Ciders (each half pint):

dry	102
sweet	119
vintage	287

Wines (each glass):

red wine	80
rose wine	83
white wine, dry	77
medium	88
sweet	110
sparkling	89

Fortified liqueur wines (each glass):

port	74
sherry, dry	55
medium	56
sweet	64

Vermouths (each glass):

dry	56
sweet	71

Liqueurs (each glass):

Advocaat	128
Cherry brandy	121
Curaçao	147

DRINK	CALS

Spirits (70% proof) (each single pub measure):
gin, rum, vodka, whisky   52

CHAPTER 21

Some Sample Menus

The 3D Diet is a 'free' diet. This means that, unlike most other diets, there are no fixed meals. Instead there are limits to the daily consumption of calories, saturated fats and cholesterol. The following menus are included simply as *examples*. They illustrate how delicious and varied your choice of dishes can be. In particular you will notice that:

* there is no need to depend on salads

* there is no need to cut out potatoes

* there is no need even to cut out alcohol.

If you think in terms of moderation you can see how easy it is to lose weight AND enjoy your food.

The menus show, for each dish, the calories, saturated fats, and cholesterol.

1,000 calories

Breakfast	Cal	S.F.	Ch.
Home-made muesli (p 53)	130	½	1
Coffee with skimmed milk†	20	½	½

Lunch			
Orange juice (225ml, 8 oz)	85	0	0
Jacket potato with Edam cheese & apple & cabbage slaw (p 122)	115	5	20
Coffee with skimmed milk	20	½	½

†All these sample menus assume coffee or tea *without* sugar but with optional artificial sweetener.

131

Supper

	Cal	S.F.	Ch.
Guacomole with crudites (p 68)	100	2	½
Beef & wine casserole (p 83)	265	2	65
Peach Melba (p 104)	100	½	9
Wine (2 glasses)	160	0	0
TOTAL	995	11	96½

1,250 calories

Breakfast

	Cal	S.F.	Ch.
Melon & orange waker (p 59)	110	½	½
Kedgeree (p 58)	165	½	65
Coffee with skimmed milk	20	½	½

Lunch

	Cal	S.F.	Ch.
Pasta & chicken salad (p 98)	235	1	40
Coffee with skimmed milk	20	½	½

Supper

	Cal	S.F.	Ch.
French onion soup (p 64)	50	½	½
Roast lamb with garlic (p 78)	300	5	90
Boiled potatoes (115g, 4 oz)	90	0	0
Broccoli (115g, 4 oz)	20	0	0
Peas (115g, 4 oz)	50	0	0
Lemon jelly with bananas (p 111)	30	½	2
Wine (2 glasses)	100	0	0
TOTAL	1250	9	199

1,500 calories

Breakfast

	Cal	S.F.	Ch.
Shredded Wheat (p 52)	120	½	1
Mushrooms & tomato on toast (p 124)	½	½	½
Tea with skimmed milk	½	½	½

Lunch

Tuna (in brine) salad (p 99)	30	2	30
1 slice wholemeal bread with St Ivel Gold	90	½	0
Coffee with skimmed milk	20	½	½

Supper

Smoked mackerel pâté (p 70)	140	4	45
1 slice wholemeal toast	60	½	0
Veal in breadcrumbs (p 86)	225	4	65
Mashed potatoes (115g, 4 oz)	135	0	0
Boiled parsnips (115g, 4 oz)	65	0	0
Sweetcorn (55g, 2 oz)	65	0	0
2 Crepes Suzette (p 108)	55	0	0
Wine (2 glasses)	160	0	0
TOTAL	1455	13½	143

CHAPTER 22

Saturated Fat Content of Some Common Foods

FOOD	TOTAL FAT g/100g	SATU-RATED g/100g
CEREALS AND CEREAL PRODUCTS		
Grains, flours and starches		
bran, wheat	5.5	1.1
flour, wholemeal	2.0	0.4
white	1.2	0.2
oatmeal	8.7	1.6
rice	1.0	0.3
bread, wholemeal	2.7	0.7
white	1.7	0.5
Biscuits		
chocolate, full-coated	27.6	17.4
crispbread, rye	2.1	0.4
wheat, starch reduced	7.6	2.8
digestive, chocolate	24.1	12.7
ginger nuts	15.2	7.5
Matzo	1.9	0.4
oatcakes	18.3	4.1
sandwich	25.9	15.2
semi-sweet	16.6	8.3
short-sweet	23.4	12.3
wafers, filled	29.9	19.4
Cakes		
fancy iced cakes	14.9	9.8
fruit cake, plain	12.9	6.1

FOOD	TOTAL FAT g/100g	SATU-RATED g/100g
Madeira cake	16.9	9.3
spongecake, jam filled	4.9	2.0

Puddings

ice cream, dairy	6.6	4.6
non-dairy	8.2	4.4
jelly, packet, cubes	0	0
made with water	0	0
made with milk	1.6	1.0
meringues	0	0

MILK AND MILK PRODUCTS

milk, cows, fresh whole	3.8	2.4
fresh skimmed	0.1	0.1
goats	4.5	3.1
human	4.1	2.0
butter, salted	82.0	51.8
cream, single	21.2	13.4
double	48.2	30.5
whipping	35.0	22.1

Cheese

Camembert type	23.2	14.7
Cheddar type	33.5	21.2
Danish Blue type	29.2	18.5
Edam type	22.9	14.5
Parmesan	29.7	18.8
Stilton	40.0	25.3
cottage cheese	4.0	2.5
cream cheese	47.4	30.0
processed cheese	25.0	15.8
cheese spread	22.9	14.5

FOOD	TOTAL FAT g/100g	SATU- RATED g/100g
Yoghurt, low-fat		
natural	1.0	0.6
flavoured	0.9	0.6
fruit	1.0	0.6
hazelnut	2.6	1.6
EGGS		
eggs, whole, raw	10.9	4.2
white, raw	trace	trace
yolk, raw	30.5	11.8
FATS AND OILS		
butter, salted	82.0	51.8
compound cooking fat	99.3	41.8
dripping, beef	99.0	44.5
lard	99.0	43.8
low fat spread	40.7	11.5
Margarine		
hard, animal and vegetable oils	81.0	31.2
vegetable oils only	81.0	31.2
soft, animal and vegetable oils	81.0	25.6
vegetable oils only	81.0	26.8
polyunsaturated, vegetable oils only	81.0	20.0
suet, shredded	86.7	51.5
Vegetable oils		
coconut	99.9	75.8
cottonseed	99.9	28.2
maize, corn	99.9	18.8
olive	99.9	15.4

FOOD	TOTAL FAT g/100g	SATU- RATED g/100g
palm	99.9	47.4
peanut, groundnut, arachis	99.9	20.5
safflower seed	99.9	11.2
soyabean	99.9	22.1
sunflower seed	99.9	14.0

MEAT (raw unless otherwise stated)

bacon, fat	80.9	35.0
lean	7.4	3.2
beef, fat	66.9	30.0
lean	4.6	2.1
lamb, fat	71.8	36.6
lean	8.8	4.6
pork, fat	71.4	30.3
lean	7.1	3.0
chicken, light meat	3.2	1.1
dark meat	5.5	1.9
duck, meat only	4.8	1.4
meat, fat and skin	42.7	12.3
grouse, roast	5.3	1.3
partridge, roast	9.3	3.3
pheasant, roast	9.3	3.3
turkey, light meat	1.1	0.4
dark meat	3.6	1.3
rabbit	4.0	1.7

Offal

brain, calf and lamb	7.6	3.1
heart, lamb	5.6	2.7
ox	3.6	2.2
kidney, lamb	2.7	1.2
ox	2.6	1.5
pig	2.7	1.2
liver, calf	7.3	3.0

FOOD	TOTAL FAT g/100g	SATU-RATED g/100g
chicken	6.3	2.7
lamb	10.3	4.3
ox	7.8	3.9
pig	6.8	2.8
sweetbread, lamb	7.8	4.0
tripe, dressed	2.5	1.5
Canned meats		
ham	5.1	2.0
ham and pork, chopped	23.6	9.2
luncheon meat	26.9	10.9
tongue	16.5	6.7
Sausages		
liver sausage	26.9	10.6
sausages, beef	24.1	10.7
pork	32.1	13.3
Other products		
steak and kidney pie	21.2	9.3

FISH (raw unless otherwise stated)

White fish		
cod	0.7	0.2
haddock	0.6	0.2
halibut	2.4	0.4
lemon sole	1.4	0.3
plaice	2.2	0.5
saithe	0.5	0.1
Fatty fish		
herring	18.5	4.1

FOOD	TOTAL FAT g/100g	SATU-RATED g/100g
mackerel	16.3	4.4
pilchards, canned in tomato sauce	5.4	1.9
salmon, canned	8.2	2.3
raw	12.0	3.3
sardines, canned in oil (fish plus oil)	28.3	5.8
canned in tomato sauce	11.6	3.6
tuna, canned in oil	22.0	4.1
Crustacea		
crab	5.2	0.9
lobster	2.4	0.6
shrimps	2.4	0.5
Molluscs		
mussels	1.9	0.5
oysters	0.9	0.3
scallops	1.4	0.5
Fish products		
roe, cod, hard	1.7	0.4

VEGETABLES AND FRUIT (raw unless otherwise stated)

Vegetables

artichokes	trace	trace
asparagus	trace	trace
beans, French	trace	trace
runner	0.2	0.1
baked, canned in tomato sauce	0.5	0.1
beansprouts, canned	trace	trace
beetroot	trace	trace

FOOD	TOTAL FAT g/100g	SATU-RATED g/100g
broccoli tops	trace	trace
brussels sprouts	trace	trace
cabbage (all types)	trace	trace
carrots	trace	trace
cauliflower	trace	trace
celeriac	trace	trace
celery	trace	trace
chicory	trace	trace
cucumber	0.1	trace
endive	trace	trace
horseradish	trace	trace
leeks	trace	trace
marrow	trace	trace
mushrooms	0.6	0.2
mustard and cress	trace	trace
okra	trace	trace
onions	trace	trace
parsley	trace	trace
parsnip	trace	trace
peas, fresh	0.4	0.1
peppers, green	0.4	0.1
potatoes	0.1	trace
pumpkin	trace	trace
radishes	trace	trace
salsify	trace	trace
seakale	trace	trace
spinach	0.5	0.1
spring greens	trace	trace
swedes	trace	trace
sweet potatoes	0.6	0.3
tomatoes, raw	trace	trace
canned	trace	trace
turnips	0.3	trace
watercress	trace	trace

FOOD	TOTAL FAT g/100g	SATU-RATED g/100g
Fruit		
avocado pears	22.2	2.7
bananas	0.3	0.1
most other fruit	trace	trace
Nuts		
almonds	53.5	4.4
Brazil nuts	64.0	17.1
chestnuts	2.7	0.5
cob or hazel nuts	36.0	2.7
coconut	36.0	32.8
peanuts	49.0	9.7
peanut butter	53.7	11.1
walnuts	51.5	5.9
CHOCOLATE PRODUCTS		
chocolate, milk	30.3	18.6
plain	29.2	18.2
cocoa powder	21.7	13.4
drinking chocolate	6.0	3.7

CHAPTER 23

Cholesterol Content of Some Common Foods

FOOD	CHOLESTEROL mg/100g
CEREAL PRODUCTS	
Cakes	
fruit cake, rich	50
rich, iced	40
gingerbread	60
rock cakes	40
spongecake, with fat	130
without fat	260
Buns and pastries	
éclairs	90
pastry, choux, raw	110
cooked	170
scones	5
Scotch pancakes	50
Puddings	
bread and butter pudding	100
cheesecake	95
Christmas pudding	60
custard, egg	100
made with powder	16
custard tart	60
dumpling	8
ice cream, dairy	21
non-dairy	11

jelly, packet, cubes	0
made with water	0
made with milk	6
lemon meringue pie	90
meringues	0
milk pudding	15
pancakes	65
Queen of puddings	100
sponge pudding, steamed	80
suet pudding, steamed	4
trifle	50
Yorkshire pudding	70

MILK AND MILK PRODUCTS
Milk

milk, cows, fresh whole	14
fresh, skimmed	2
human	16
butter, salted	230
cream, single	66
double	140
whipping	100

Cheese

Camembert type	72
Cheddar type	70
Danish Blue type	88
Edam type	72
Parmesan	90
Stilton	120
cottage cheese	13
cream cheese	94
processed cheese	88
cheese spread	71

Yoghurt, low-fat

natural	7
flavoured	7
fruit	6
hazelnut	7

EGGS AND EGG PRODUCTS

Eggs

whole, raw	450
white, raw	0
yolk, raw	1260
dried	1780
boiled	450
poached	480
omelette	410
scrambled	410

Egg and cheese dishes

cauliflower cheese	17
cheese pudding	130
cheese soufflé	180
macaroni cheese	20
pizza, cheese and tomato	20
Quiche Lorraine	130
Scotch egg	220
Welsh rarebit	67

Products containing eggs

lemon curd, home-made	150
marzipan, home-made	35
mayonnaise, home-made	260

FATS AND OILS

dripping, beef	60
lard	70
low-fat spread	trace
suet, block	60
shredded	74
vegetable oils	trace

MEAT (raw unless otherwise stated)

bacon, lean and fat	57
lean only	51
beef, lean and fat	65
lean only	59
lamb, lean and fat	78
lean only	79
pork, lean and fat	72
lean only	69
chicken, light meat	69
dark meat	
duck, meat only	110
turkey, light meat	49
dark meat	81
rabbit	71

Offal

brain, calf and lamb	2200
heart, lamb	140
ox	140
kidney, lamb	400
ox	400
pig	410
liver, calf	370

chicken	380
lamb	430
ox	270
pig	260
oxtail	75
sweetbread, lamb	260
tongue, lamb	180
ox, pickled	78
tripe, dressed	95

MEAT PRODUCTS AND DISHES

Canned meats

beef, corned	85
ham	33
ham and pork, chopped	60
luncheon meat	53
stewed steak with gravy	44
tongue	110
veal, jellied	97

Offal products

black pudding, fried	68
faggots	79
haggis, boiled	91
liver sausage	120

Sausages

Frankfurters	46
polony	40
salami	79
sausages, beef	40
pork	47
saveloy	45

FOOD	CHOLESTEROL mg/100g

Other products

beefburgers, frozen	59
brawn	52
meat paste	68

Meat and pastry products

Cornish pastie	49
pork pie, individual	52
sausage roll, flaky pastry	20
short pastry	30
steak and kidney pie, pastry top only	125

Cooked dishes

beef steak pudding	30
beef stew	30
Bolognese sauce	25
curried meat	25
hot pot	25
Irish stew	35
moussaka	40
shepherd's pie	25

FISH (raw unless otherwise stated)

White fish

cod	50
haddock	60
halibut	50
lemon sole	60
plaice	70

FOOD	CHOLESTEROL mg/100g
saithe	60
whiting, steamed	110

Fatty fish
herring	70
kipper, baked	80
mackerel	80
pilchards, canned in tomato sauce	70
salmon, raw	70
canned	90
smoked	70
sardines, canned in oil	
fish only	100
fish plus oil	80
canned in tomato sauce	100
trout, steamed	80
tuna, canned in oil	65

Crustacea
crab, fresh	100
canned	100
lobster	150
prawns	200
scampi	110
shrimps	200

Molluscs
cockles	40
mussels	100
oysters	50
scallops	40

FOOD	CHOLESTEROL mg/100g
whelks	100
winkles	100
Fish products and dishes	
fish fingers	50
fish pie	20
kedgeree	120
roe, cod, hard	500
herring, soft	700

CHAPTER 24

Calorie Counter

CEREALS AND CEREAL PRODUCTS

Grains, flours and starches

Flour, wholemeal	318
white, plain	350
Macaroni, raw	370
boiled	117
Porridge	44
Rice, raw	361
boiled	123
Spaghetti, raw	378
boiled	117
canned in tomato sauce	59

Bread and rolls

Bread	
wholemeal	216
white	233
Rolls, brown	285
white	302
starch reduced	384

Breakfast cereals

All-Bran	273
Cornflakes	368
Grapenuts	355

Muesli	368
Puffed Wheat	325
Ready Brek	390
Rice Krispies	372
Shredded Wheat	324
Special K	388
Sugar Puffs	348
Weetabix	340

Biscuits

Chocolate, full-coated	524
Cream crackers	440
Crispbread	321
starch reduced	388
Digestive, plain	471
chocolate	493
Matzo	384
Shortbread	504

Cakes

Fancy iced cakes	407
Fruit cake	354
Gingerbread	373
Madeira cake	393
Rock cakes	394
Sponge cake	464

Buns and pastries

Doughnuts	349
Eclairs	376
Jam tarts	384
Mince pies	435
Pastry, choux, cooked	330
Pastry, flaked, cooked	565
Pastry, shortcrust, cooked	527

Scones	371
Scotch pancakes	283

Puddings

Apple crumble	208
Bread and butter pudding	159
Cheesecake	421
Christmas pudding	304
Custard, egg	118
Dumpling	211
Ice cream	166
Jelly, made with water	59
Lemon meringue pie	323
Meringues	380
Milk pudding	131
Pancakes (traditional recipe)	307
Sponge pudding	344
Trifle (traditional recipe)	160
Yorkshire pudding (traditional recipe)	215

MILK AND MILK PRODUCTS

Milk

cows, whole	65
skimmed	33
butter	740

Cream

single	212
double	447
whipping	332

Cheese

Camembert type	300

	Calories per 100g food
Cheddar type	406
Danish Blue type	355
Edam type	304
Parmesan	408
Stilton	462
cottage cheese	96
cream cheese	439
processed cheese	311
cheese spread	283

Yoghurt, low-fat

natural	52
flavoured	81
fruit	95
hazelnut	106

EGGS

Eggs

whole, raw	147
white, raw	36
yolk, raw	339
boiled	147
fried	232
poached	155
omelette	190
scrambled	246

Egg and cheese dishes

cheese soufflé	252
pizza, cheese and tomato	234
Quiche Lorraine	391
Scotch egg	279
Welsh rarebit	365

FATS AND OILS

Butter	740
Cod liver oil	899
Dripping, beef	891
Lard	891
Low fat spread	366
Margarine	730
Suet, shredded	826
Vegetable oils	899

MEAT AND MEAT PRODUCTS

Bacon

gammon, joint,	
boiled, lean and fat	236
lean only	167
rashers, fried	
lean only	332
back, lean and fat	465
middle, lean and fat	477
streaky, lean and fat	496
rashers, grilled	
lean only	292
back, lean and fat	405
middle, lean and fat	416
streaky, lean and fat	422

Beef

mince, stewed	229
rump steak, fried, lean and fat	246
lean only	190
grilled, lean and fat	218
lean only	168

	Calories per 100g food
sirloin, roast, lean and fat	284
lean only	192

Lamb

chops, grilled, lean and fat	277
lean only	222
leg, roast, lean and fat	266
lean only	191
shoulder, roast, lean and fat	316
lean only	196

Pork

chops, grilled, lean and fat	258
lean only	133
leg, roast, lean and fat	286
lean only	185

Veal

cutlet, fried	215

Poultry and game

Chicken, roast, meat and skin	216
light meat	142
dark meat	155
Duck, roast, meat, fat and skin	339
meat only	189
Turkey, roast, meat and skin	171
light meat	132
dark meat	148

Offal

Brain	139
Heart, roast	237
stewed	179

Kidneys, fried	155
stewed	153
Liver, calf, raw	153
fried	254
chicken, raw	135
fried	194
lamb, raw	179
fried	232
Sweetbread, raw	131
fried	230
Tongue, boiled	293

Meat products and dishes

Canned meats
Beef, corned	217
Ham	120
Luncheon meat	313
Stewed steak with gravy	176
Tongue	213

Offal products
Black pudding, fried	305
Haggis, boiled	310
Liver sausage	310

Sausages
Frankfurters	274
Polony	281
Salami	491
Sausages, beef	267
pork	317
Beefburgers	264
Meat paste	173

	Calories per 100g food

Meat and pastry products

Cornish pastie	332
Pork pie	376
Sausage roll	471
Steak and kidney pie, pastry top only	286
individual	323

Cooked dishes (traditional recipes)

Bolognese sauce	139
Hot pot	114
Irish stew	124
Moussaka	195
Shepherd's pie	119

FISH AND FISH PRODUCTS

White fish

Cod, fried in batter	199
grilled	95
steamed	83
Haddock, fried	174
steamed	98
smoked, steamed	101
Halibut, steamed	131
Lemon sole, fried	216
steamed	91
Plaice, fried in batter	279
fried in crumbs	228
steamed	93
Whiting, fried	191
steamed	92

Fatty fish

Herring, raw	234

	Calories per 100g food
Kipper, baked	205
baked (weighed with bones)	111
Mackerel, raw	223
fried	188
Pilchards, canned in tomato sauce	126
Salmon, steamed	197
canned	155
smoked	142
Sardines, canned in oil, fish only	217
fish plus oil	334
canned in tomato sauce	177
Trout, steamed	135
Tuna, canned in oil	289
Whitebait, fried	525

Crustacea

Crab, boiled	127
boiled (weighed with shell)	25
canned	81
Lobster, boiled	119
boiled (weighed with shell)	42
Prawns, boiled	107
boiled (weighed with shell)	41
Scampi, fried	316
Shrimps, boiled	117
boiled (weighed with shell)	39
canned	94

Molluscs

Cockles, boiled	48
Mussels, boiled	87
boiled (weighed with shell)	26
Oysters, raw	51
raw (weighed with shell)	6
Scallops, steamed	105

Fish products and dishes

Fish cakes, frozen	112
fried	188
Fish fingers, frozen	178
fried	233
Fish paste	169
Kedgeree (traditional recipe)	151
Roe, cod, raw	113

VEGETABLES

Artichokes	16
Asparagus	18
Aubergine	14
Beans	
French, boiled	7
runner, boiled	19
broad, boiled	48
butter, raw	273
boiled	95
haricot, raw	271
boiled	93
baked, canned in tomato sauce	64
red kidney, raw	272
canned or cooked	93
Beansprouts	9
Beetroot, boiled	44
Broccoli tops, boiled	18
Brussels sprouts, boiled	18
Cabbage, boiled	10
Carrots, boiled	20
Cauliflower, boiled	9
Celery, raw	8
Cucumber, raw	10

Leeks, boiled	24
Lentils, raw	304
split, boiled	99
Lettuce, raw	12
Marrow, boiled	7
Mushrooms, raw	13
fried	210
Onions, raw	23
boiled	13
fried	345
spring, raw	35
Parsley, raw	21
Parsnips, boiled	56
Peas, boiled	46
Peas, chick, raw	320
Peppers, green, raw	15
Potatoes, boiled	78
mashed	119
baked	105
baked (weighed with skins)	85
roast	157
chips	253
crisps	533
Radishes, raw	15
Spinach, boiled	30
Spring greens, boiled	10
Swedes, boiled	18
Sweetcorn, boiled	123
Tomatoes, raw	14
fried	69
canned	12
Turnips, boiled	14

FRUIT

Apples	46
Apricots	28
Avocado pears	223
Bananas	79
Blackberries	29
Cherries	47
Currants, dried	243
Damsons	38
Dates, dried	248
Figs, raw	41
dried	213
Gooseberries	17
Grapes	62
Grapefruit, raw	22
canned	60
Greengages	47
Lemons, whole	15
juice, fresh	7
Mandarin oranges, canned	56
Mangoes	59
Melons	22
watermelon	21
Olives, in brine	103
Oranges, raw	35
juice, fresh	38
Peaches, fresh	37
canned	87
Pears	41
Pineapples, fresh	46
canned	77
Plums	38
Prunes, dried	161
Raisins, dried	246

	Calories per 100g food
Raspberries, raw	25
canned	87
Rhubarb	6
Strawberries, raw	26
canned	81
Sultanas, dried	250
Tangerines	34

NUTS

Almonds	565
Brazil nuts	619
Chestnuts	170
Cob or hazel nuts	380
Coconut, fresh	351
desiccated	604
Peanuts, fresh	570
roasted and salted	570
Peanut butter, smooth	623
Walnuts	525

SUGARS AND PRESERVES

Sugars
Sugar	394
Syrup, golden	298
Treacle, black	257

Preserves
Honey	288
Jam	261
Lemon curd	286
Marmalade	261
Marzipan	443
Mincemeat	235

CONFECTIONERY

Boiled sweets	327
Chocolate, milk	529
plain	525
Mars bar	441
Fruit gums	172
Liquorice allsorts	313

BEVERAGES

Bournvita	377
Cocoa powder	312
Coffee, ground	287
infusion	2
instant	100
Drinking chocolate	366
Horlicks malted milk	396
Ovaltine	378
Tea	108
infusion	1

SOFT DRINKS, FRUIT AND VEGETABLE JUICES

Coca-cola	39
Grapefruit juice, canned, unsweetened	31
sweetened	38
Lemonade, bottled	21
Lime juice cordial, undiluted	112
Lucozade	68
Orange drink, undiluted	112
Orange juice, canned, unsweetened	33
sweetened	51

Pineapple juice, canned	53
Ribena, undiluted	229
Rosehip syrup, undiluted	232
Tomato juice, canned	16

ALCHOLIC BEVERAGES

See Chapter 20

SAUCES AND PICKLES

Bread sauce	110
Brown sauce, bottled	99
Chutney, apple	193
tomato	154
French dressing	658
Mayonnaise	718
Piccalilli	33
Salad cream	311
Tomato ketchup	98
Tomato puree	67
Tomato sauce	86

SOUPS (as served, canned or traditional recipes)

Chicken, cream of	58
Chicken noodle	20
Lentil	99
Minestrone	23
Mushroom, cream of	53
Oxtail	44
Tomato, cream of	55
Vegetable	37

FOODS WITH NO OR NEGLIGIBLE CALORIES

Tea without milk, cream or sugar
Coffee without milk, cream or sugar
Plain water
Carbonated water
Mineral water
Low-calorie squashes
Low-calorie carbonated drinks
Artificial sweeteners
Salt
Pepper
Mustard
Garlic
Curry powder
Lemons and lemon juice
Vinegar

CHAPTER 25

Height and Weight Tables

Maximum desirable weights for adults
(irrespective of age)

Height without shoes			Weight from			to		
ft	in	cm	st	lb	kg	st	lb	kg

MEN

ft	in	cm	st	lb	kg	st	lb	kg
5	3	160.0	9	2	58.1	10	10	68.0
5	4	162.6	9	5	59.4	11	0	69.9
5	5	165.1	9	9	61.2	12	4	71.7
5	6	167.6	9	13	63.0	11	9	73.9
5	7	170.2	10	3	64.9	12	0	76.2
5	8	172.7	10	7	66.7	12	4	78.0
5	9	175.3	10	12	68.9	12	8	79.8
5	10	177.8	11	2	70.8	12	13	82.1
5	11	180.3	11	6	72.6	13	40	84.4
6	0	182.9	11	10	74 4	13	9	86.6
6	1	185.4	12	1	76.7	14	0	88.9
6	2	188.0	12	5	78.5	14	5	91.2
6	3	190.5	12	9	80.3	14	10	93.4

Maximum desirable weights for adults
(irrespective of age)

Height without shoes			Weight from			to		
ft	in	cm	st	lb	kg	st	lb	kg

WOMEN

4	11	149.9	7	10	49.0	9	3	58.5
5	0	152.4	7	11	49.4	9	6	59.9
5	1	154.9	8	2	51.7	9	9	61.2
5	2	157.5	8	5	53.1	9	13	63.0
5	3	160.0	8	8	54.4	10	3	64.9
5	4	162.6	8	12	56.2	10	7	66.7
5	5	165.1	9	2	58.1	10	11	68.5
5	6	167.6	9	6	59.9	11	1	70.3
5	7	170.2	9	10	61.7	11	5	72.1
5	8	172.7	10	1	64.0	11	10	74.4
5	9	175.3	10	5	65.8	12	1	76.7
5	10	177.8	10	9	67.6	12	7	79.4

The weights include indoor clothes and shoes (without clothes and shoes subtract 10 lb or 4.7 kg for men and 6 lb or 2.7 kg for women).

Note on use of table of Maximum Desirable Weights:
The table shows the *range* of weights for each height. Some books and magazines indicate weights for different frame sizes – small, medium and large. The problem is that no reliable method has yet been devised to determine whether your frame is in fact small, medium or large. Various methods have been described using such criteria as wrist circumference and shoe size, but these are often inaccurate guides to frame size. The only way to decide which build you are is to look at yourself in a mirror (but not through rose-tinted spectacles!) and, perhaps with the help of your

husband or wife or other relative or friend, make up your mind about it. You can then judge whereabouts in the range of weights you should fit. If, without clothes, you look broad-shouldered and muscular your weight should be around the upper end of the range; if you look narrow-shouldered and not muscular your weight should be around the lower end of the range for your height. Most people fit somewhere in the middle which is where to place yourself if in doubt.

Range of heights and weights — boys

Age (yrs)	Height from ft	in	to ft	in	Height from cm	top cm	Weight from st	lb	to st	lb	Weight from kg	to kg
Birth	1	7½	1	11	50.2	57.8		5½		9½	2.5	4.4
¼	1	10½	2	1½	56.6	64.7		10		16½	4.7	7.4
½	2	1	2	4½	63.8	72.6	1	0	1	8	6.4	9.9
¾	2	2½	2	6½	67.9	77.4	1	2½	1	11	7.5	11.5
1	2	4	2	8	71.2	81.4	1	4½	1	13½	8.3	12.6
1¼	2	5	2	9½	74.0	84.7	1	5½	2	1½	8.9	13.5
1½	2	6	2	10½	76.5	87.8	1	6½	2	3½	9.4	14.3
1¾	2	7	2	11½	78.7	90.5	1	7½	2	5	9.8	14.9
2	2	8	3	0½	80.7	93.1	1	8½	2	6½	10.2	15.6
2½	2	9	3	2	83.5	96.9	1	10	2	9	10.9	16.9
3	2	10½	3	4	87.0	101.4	1	12	2	12	11.6	18.0
3½	2	11½	3	5½	90.4	105.7	1	13	3	0	12.3	19.2
4	3	1	3	7	93.5	109.7	2	1	3	3	13.0	20.4
4½	3	2	3	8½	96.5	113.5	2	2	3	6	13.7	21.8
5	3	3	3	10	99.4	117.2	2	4	3	9	14.4	23.2
5½	3	4½	3	11½	102.2	120.8	2	5	3	13	15.1	24.8
6	3	5½	4	1	104.9	124.3	2	7	4	2	15.9	26.5
6½	3	6½	4	2½	107.6	127.6	2	9	4	6	16.6	28.3
7	3	7½	4	3½	110.3	130.8	2	11	4	11	17.4	30.3
7½	3	8½	4	4½	112.9	133.9	2	12	5	1	18.2	32.3
8	3	9½	4	6	115.4	137.0	3	0	5	6	19.1	34.4
8½	3	10½	4	7	117.9	139.9	3	2	5	10	20.0	36.5
9	3	11½	4	8½	120.4	142.9	3	4	6	1	21.0	38.8
9½	4	0½	4	9½	122.8	145.8	3	6	6	6	21.9	41.0
10	4	1½	4	10½	125.1	148.5	3	8	6	11	23.0	43.3
10½	4	2½	4	11½	127.2	151.4	3	11	7	4	24.0	46.3
11	4	3	5	1	129.4	154.4	3	13	7	11	24.9	49.3
11½	4	4	5	2	131.7	157.8	4	1	8	5	26.0	53.3
12	4	4½	5	3½	133.7	160.9	4	4	9	0	27.1	57.2
12½	4	5½	5	4½	136.3	164.4	4	6	9	8	28.1	61.0
13	4	6½	5	6	138.7	168.2	4	9	10	2	29.6	64.4
13½	4	7½	5	7½	141.5	172.0	4	13	10	9	31.2	67.8
14	4	9	5	9½	145.0	176.2	5	3	11	2	33.3	70.9
14½	4	10½	5	10½	148.4	179.6	5	9	11	8	36.0	73.7
15	5	0	6	0	152.3	182.4	6	2	11	13	39.0	75.9
15½	5	1	6	0½	155.9	184.3	6	10	12	2	42.7	77.5
16	5	2½	6	1	158.9	185.5	7	3	12	5	45.7	78.6
16½	5	3½	6	1½	160.7	186.2	7	6	12	7	47.5	79.5
17	5	3½	6	1½	161.7	186.8	7	9	12	8	48.6	80.2
18	5	4	6	1½	162.2	187.2	7	12	12	10	50.0	81.0
19	5	4	6	1½	162.2	187.2	7	13	12	12	50.4	81.6

Range of heights and weights — girls

Age (yrs)	Height from ft	in	to ft	in	Height from cm	top cm	Weight from st	lb	to st	lb	Weight from kg	to kg
Birth	1	7½	1	10½	49.2	56.8		5½		9½	2.6	4.4
¼	1	9½	2	1	54.9	63.1		9½	1	1	4.4	6.9
½	2	0	2	3½	61.1	69.9		13	1	6	5.9	9.1
¾	2	2	2	5½	65.5	74.9	1	1½	1	9½	7.0	10.6
1	2	3	2	7	69.1	79.3	1	3	1	12	7.8	11.8
1¼	2	4½	2	8½	72.2	82.9	1	4½	2	0	8.3	12.7
1½	2	5½	2	10	74.9	86.2	1	5½	2	1½	8.9	13.5
1¾	2	6½	2	11	77.2	89.1	1	6½	2	3½	9.3	14.3
2	2	7½	3	0	79.4	91.8	1	7½	2	5	9.7	14.9
2½	2	8½	3	1½	82.2	95.6	1	9	2	8	10.5	16.3
3	2	9½	3	3½	85.7	100.2	1	11	2	11	11.4	17.6
3½	2	11	3	5	89.2	104.5	1	13	3	0	12.2	18.9
4	3	0½	3	6½	92.3	108.5	2	1	3	3	13.1	20.3
4½	3	1½	3	8½	95.4	112.4	2	2	3	6	13.8	21.8
5	3	2½	3	9½	98.2	116.1	2	4	3	9	14.6	23.3
5½	3	4	3	11	101.0	119.6	2	6	3	13	15.4	25.0
6	3	5	4	0½	103.8	123.1	2	8	4	3	16.2	26.8
6½	3	6	4	2	106.4	126.4	2	9	4	7	17.0	28.5
7	3	7	4	3	109.1	129.6	2	11	4	11	17.8	30.6
7½	3	8	4	4½	117.7	132.8	2	13	5	2	18.6	32.6
8	3	9	4	5½	114.2	135.8	3	1	5	7	19.4	35.0
8½	3	10	4	6½	116.7	138.8	3	2	5	13	20.2	37.7
9	3	11	4	8	119.3	141.9	3	4	6	5	21.0	40.6
9½	4	0	4	9	121.9	145.0	3	6	6	12	21.8	43.8
10	4	1	4	10½	124.5	148.3	3	8	7	7	22.7	47.7
10½	4	2	5	0	127.1	151.8	3	10	8	2	23.6	51.7
11	4	3	5	1½	129.5	155.8	3	12	8	11	24.7	55.7
11½	4	4	5	3	132.0	160 1	4	2	9,	5	26.2	59.6
12	4	5	5	4½	135.0	163.6	4	5	9	13	27.8	63.9
12½	4	6½	5	5½	139.0	166.1	4	9	10	6	29.7	66.5
13	4	8	5	6½	142.6	168.5	5	0	10	12	32.0	69.3
13½	4	9	5	7	144.4	170.3	5	6	11	2	34.5	71.1
14	4	10	5	7½	147.6	171.6	5	11	11	5	37.0	72.3
14½	4	11	5	8	149.4	172.7	6	3	11	7	39.5	73.2
15	4	11	5	8	150.3	173.2	6	8	11	8	41.7	73.7
15½	4	11½	5	8½	150.6	173.4	6	12	11	9	43.5	74.1
16	4	11½	5	8½	150.9	173.5	7	0	11	10	44.6	74.5
17	4	11½	5	8½	150.9	173.5	7	3	11	11	45.7	74.9
18	4	11½	5	8½	150.9	173.5	7	3	11	11	46.0	75.0
19	4	11½	5	8½	150.9	173.5	7	3	11	11	46.1	75.1

The heights and weights indicated cover ninety-four per cent of children; that is, three per cent of children will be shorter and lighter and three per cent will be taller and heavier than the range shown. When using these tables you should remember that a short child should have a weight at the lower end of the range, similarly a tall child will have a weight at the upper end of the range.

Index of Recipes

174